America's Container Ports:

Freight Hubs That Connect Our Nation to Global Markets

June 2009

U.S. Department of Transportation
Research and Innovative Technology Administration
Bureau of Transportation Statistics

**Research and Innovative Technology Administration
Bureau of Transportation Statistics**

**To obtain *America's Container Ports, 2009*
and other BTS publications**

Mail: Product Orders
            Research and Innovative Technology Administration
            Bureau of Transportation Statistics
            U.S. Department of Transportation
            1200 New Jersey Avenue, SE
            Washington, DC 20590

Internet: www.bts.gov

BTS Information Service
E-mail: answers@bts.gov
Phone: 800-853-1351

Cover photos by Chester Ford

Acknowledgments

U.S. Department of Transportation

Ray LaHood
Secretary

Research and Innovative Technology Administration

Peter H. Appel
Administrator

Bureau of Transportation Statistics

Steven K. Smith, Ph.D.
Acting Director

Produced under the direction of:
Deborah D. Johnson
Assistant Director, Office of Transportation Analysis

Project Manager
Long X. Nguyen

Major Contributors
Felix Ammah-Tagoe
E-Ternational

Shana Johnson
E-Ternational

Other Contributors
Steve Beningo
Matt Chambers
Jacob Hommeland
Gail Perkins

RITA Editor
William H. Moore

RITA Visual Information Specialist
Alpha Wingfield

Table of Contents

Overview

The U.S. marine transportation system continues to handle large volumes of domestic and international freight in support of the nation's economic activities. The demand for freight transportation responds to trends in global economic activity and merchandise trade. When U.S. businesses produce more goods, the demand for freight transportation services to move raw materials and finished products to markets and customers around the country and world will increase. When economic conditions result in less production, the demand for transportation services will decrease.

This report provides an overview of the movement of maritime freight handled by the nation's container seaports in 2008 and summarizes trends in maritime freight movement since 1995. It covers the impact of the recent U.S. and global economic downturn on U.S. port container traffic, trends in container throughput, concentration of containerized cargo at the top U.S. ports, regional shifts in cargo handled, vessel calls and capacity in ports, the rankings of U.S. ports among the world's top ports, and the number of maritime container entries into the United States relative to truck and rail containers. The report also presents snapshots of landside access to container ports, port security initiatives, and ongoing maritime environmental issues.

The principal findings of the report include the following:

- Maritime freight handled by U.S. container ports fell sharply towards the end of 2008, and the decline continued into the first quarter of 2009. Total U.S. containerized cargo for December 2008 was down 18 percent compared with December 2007. The decline was severe at the nation's two leading container ports, Los Angeles and Long Beach, which experienced 13 and 25 percent drops, respectively.

- Overall in 2008, U.S. container ports handled 28.2 million loaded TEUs (20-foot equivalent units—a measure for counting containers), a 3 percent drop from the 29 million TEUs handled in 2007.

- In 2008, containerized freight throughput fell for each of the leading ports in the Pacific/west coast, Atlantic/east coast, and gulf coast regions. West coast ports had a 5 percent decline, east coast ports a less than 1 percent decline, and gulf coast ports a 3 percent decline.

- The consequences of the 2008 decline in container throughput at the nation's seaports reached beyond the marine ports and terminals, affecting containership fleet capacity, the railroads and commercial trucks that service the seaports, and the inland warehouses and distribution centers that provide logistical support for the entire multimodal freight supply chain.

- In 2008, the decline in maritime containerized cargo impacted international intermodal containers handled by the nation's Class I railroads, which fell 7 percent from 2007. It also affected overall trucking activity, which saw record declines in the second half of 2008.

- Despite the 2007 to 2008 declines, today 1 container in every 10 that is engaged in global trade is either bound for or originates in the United States, accounting for 10 percent of worldwide container traffic.

- On a typical day in 2008, U.S. container ports handled an average of 77,000 TEUs, up from 37,000 TEUs per day in 1995.

- In 2008, the top 10 U.S. container ports accounted for 86 percent of containerized TEU imports and exports, up from 78 percent in 1995.

- In 2008, 3 U.S. ports—Los Angeles, Long Beach, and New York/New Jersey—ranked among the world's top 20 container ports when measured by TEUs, placing 16th, 17th, and 20th, respectively.

- In 2007, there were nearly 20,000 containership calls at U.S. seaports, accounting for 31 percent of the total oceangoing vessel calls made by all vessel types at U.S. ports.

- In 2007, there were about 12 million oceanborne container entries into the United States, down slightly from 2006 but still double those of 2000.

- In April 2009, a U.S.-flagged container vessel with 20 American sailors was hijacked by pirates off the coast of Somalia, highlighting the challenge of fully securing maritime cargo throughout the entire global logistics supply chain.

Introduction

America's container ports play an important role in handling U.S. merchandise trade moving to and from distant places around the world. Each year, these seaports handle exports produced at U.S. factories and farms and imports of goods such as automobiles, machinery, electronics, apparel, shoes, toys, and food. American households depend on the nation's container seaports for everyday items, and American businesses depend on these seaports for facilitating the exchange of merchandise with trading partners around the world.

During 2008, the volume of maritime freight handled by America's container ports dropped. U.S. international merchandise trade transported by maritime container vessels fell sharply toward the end of the year, a decline that continued into 2009. Total U.S. containerized freight for December 2008 was down 18 percent compared with December 2007 (table 1). Maritime containerized imports declined 15 percent, and exports fell by 21 percent (JOC PIERS 2009a). This happened as U.S. businesses cut inventories, manufacturing and construction activities stalled, and Americans cut back on spending as unemployment rose, home values fell, and investment portfolios shrank.

2008 was an exceptionally challenging year for the nation's container ports as TEU throughput dropped nationwide.

The year 2008 was exceptionally challenging for the nation's leading container seaports. After a steady pace at the beginning of the year, by end of 2008, containerized freight throughput declined for each of the leading ports in the Pacific/west coast, Atlantic/east coast, and gulf coast regions (table 1). All the major ports saw a decline in December 2008 compared with the same month in the previous year. The nation's two leading container ports, Los Angeles and Long Beach, experienced 13 and 25 percent year-on-year drops, respectively. Other leading ports saw worse declines in container traffic, with cargo falling by more than one-third to almost one-half—for example, Seattle fell 38 percent and Mobile fell 49 percent.

By the end of 2008, U.S. total maritime container traffic at all U.S. ports was estimated at 28.2 million TEUs (see box), a 3 percent drop from the 29 million TEUs in 2007 (table 1). During 2008, west coast ports had a 5 percent decline in container traffic and gulf coast ports had a 3 percent decline. East coast ports had a 0.2 percent, or essentially negligible, increase. Among the nation's top 10 leading container ports, 7 saw declines in their container cargo throughput in 2008. The two largest declines were Seattle at 16 percent and Long Beach at 8 percent (table 1 and figure 1). Only 3 of the top 10 ports, all on the east coast, handled slightly more container cargo in 2008 than in 2007—Savannah grew by 3.6 percent, New York/New Jersey by 1.4 percent, and Norfolk by 1.2 percent. These east coast ports tend to have a more diversified trade market with Europe, Asia, Latin America, and South America, unlike the west coast ports, which trade almost exclusively with the Asia-Pacific market.

TEU Defined:

The standard measure for counting containers is the 20-foot equivalent unit, or TEU. This measure is used to count containers of various lengths. A standard 40-foot container is 2 TEUs, and a 48-foot container equals 2.4 TEUs. It is also used to describe the capacities of containerships or ports.

Containerized trade between the United States and the rest of the world fell in 2008 because of the combined influence of weak domestic consumer demand, which cut import levels, and the global economic slowdown, which cut foreign demand for U.S. exports. During the second half of 2008, as the U.S. financial crisis began to directly impact consumer spending, Americans cut back on their purchase of imported clothes, automobiles, and other consumer merchandise, such as toys and flat-panel televisions. In addition, as the domestic financial crisis deepened and the global recession widened, overseas trading partners' demand for U.S. goods started to tumble, further weakening

TABLE 1
Maritime Container Cargo Handled at Leading U.S. Container Ports: 2007 and 2008
(Thousands of TEUs)

Ranked within port region	Monthly comparison, December 2007 and December 2008			Annual comparison, 2007 and 2008		
	December 2007	December 2008	Percent change from same month previous year	2007	2008	Percent change from previous year
West coast total	1,177	939	-20.2	14,906	14,162	-5.0
Los Angeles, CA	450	393	-12.6	5,740	5,671	-1.2
Long Beach, CA	391	294	-24.8	4,995	4,612	-7.7
Oakland, CA	115	95	-17.3	1,451	1,395	-3.9
Tacoma, WA	93	71	-23.4	1,151	1,129	-1.9
Seattle, WA	106	66	-37.7	1,289	1,083	-16.0
Other ports	22	20	-9.8	280	273	-2.4
East coast total	976	820	-16.0	12,011	12,030	0.2
New York/New Jersey	316	279	-11.7	3,935	3,992	1.4
Savannah, GA	162	138	-14.9	2,042	2,116	3.6
Norfolk, VA	131	104	-20.4	1,573	1,592	1.2
Charleston, SC	111	81	-27.1	1,408	1,331	-5.5
Port Everglades, FL	59	48	-18.3	692	681	-1.6
Miami, FL	57	47	-18.4	685	669	-2.3
Wilmington, NC	16	9	-41.6	150	147	-1.8
Other ports	126	115	-8.5	1,526	1,502	-1.6
Gulf coast total	165	147	-11.1	2,052	1,998	-2.6
Houston, TX	115	104	-9.3	1,416	1,371	-3.2
Mobile, AL	7	4	-48.8	68	75	10.4
Other ports	43	39	-9.7	568	552	-2.8
U.S. total TEUs	2,318	1,906	-17.8	28,969	28,190	-2.7

KEY: TEUs = twenty-foot equivalent units. One 20-foot container equals one TEU, and one 40-foot container equals two TEUs.

SOURCE: U.S. Department of Transportation, Research and Innovative Technology Administration, Bureau of Transportation Statistics, based on data from *The Journal of Commerce*, Port Import Export Reporting Service (PIERS), reported by Georgia Ports Authority in U.S. Port Rankings report, available at http://www.gaports.com/SalesandMarketing/MarketingBusinessDevelopment/GPABytheNumbers/tabid/435/Default.aspx as of Feb. 16, 2009.

the maritime container market. As a result, declines occurred in U.S. demand for maritime container transportation by ocean vessels, cargo-handling activity at the container ports, and the volume of intermodal freight moved to and from the ports by truck and rail.

The declines in maritime container traffic mirrored the slide in overall U.S. international merchandise exports and imports transported by all modes of transportation in 2007 and 2008 and followed the trend in the national economy as a whole (figure 2 and figure 3). According to the U.S. Department of Commerce, the primary contributors to the

declines in merchandise exports and imports in the fourth quarter of 2008 were industrial supplies and materials; automotive vehicles, parts, and engines; consumer goods; and foods, feeds, and beverages (USDOC CB BEA 2009). When adjusted for inflation, the value of merchandise exports in the fourth quarter of 2008 dropped 34 percent compared with that of the third quarter. The value of merchandise imports dropped 19 percent (figure 3).

Trends in container shipping are directly related to patterns in overall international trade, which is a primary contributing factor in the nation's economic growth. For example, real gross domestic

FIGURE 1
Maritime Container Cargo Handled at Top 10 U.S. Container Ports: 2007 and 2008
(Millions of TEUs)

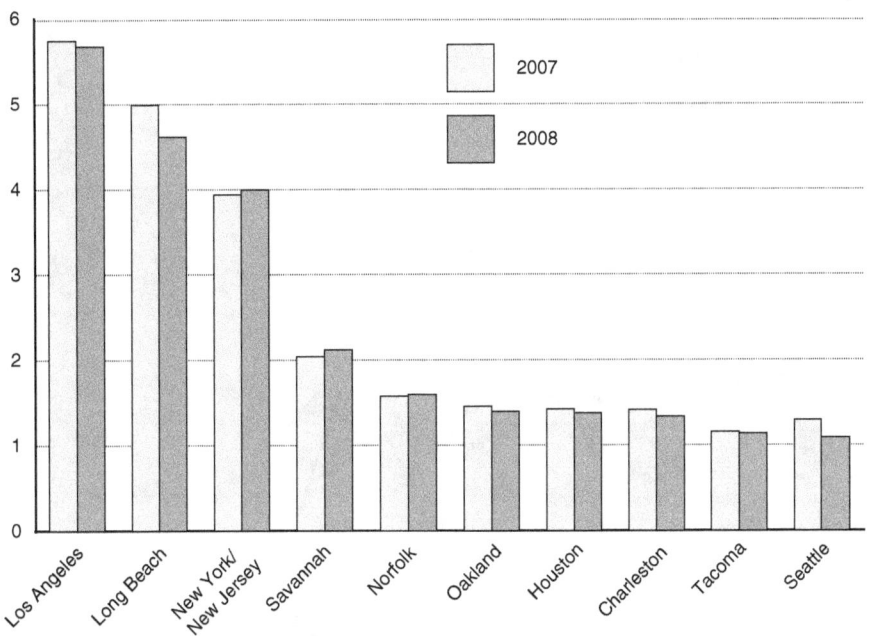

SOURCE: U.S. Department of Transportation, Research and Innovative Technology Administration, Bureau of Transportation Statistics, based on data from *The Journal of Commerce*, Port Import Export Reporting Service (PIERS), reported by Georgia Ports Authority in U.S. Port Rankings report, available at http://www.gaports.com/SalesandMarketing/Marketing-BusinessDevelopment/GPABytheNumbers/tabid/435/Default.aspx as of January 2009.

FIGURE 2
Quarterly Value of Total U.S. International Merchandise Trade: 2007 and 2008
(Billions of chained 2000 dollars)

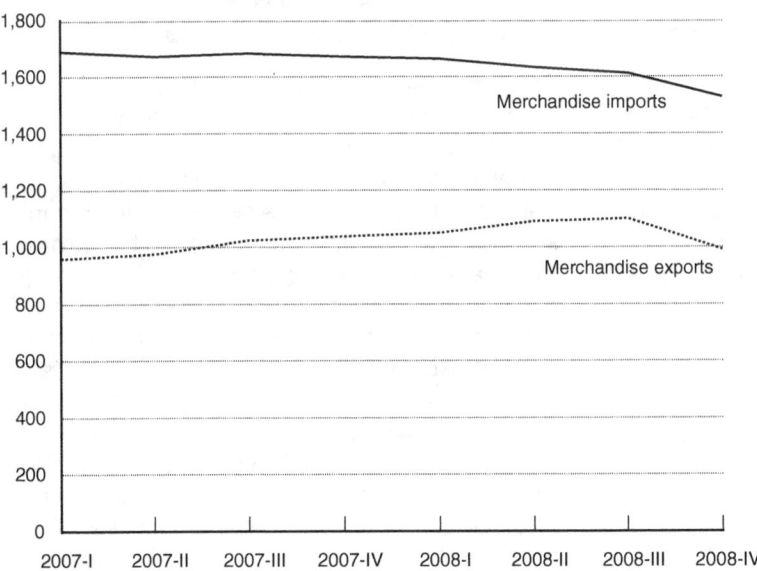

NOTE: To compare economic changes over time, current or nominal values of currencies are adjusted for inflation. In the United States, the Bureau of Economic Analysis establishes indices to calculate changes between years. These are used to calculate real chained dollars. Annual changes in the indices are chained (multiplied) together to form a time series. Chained dollars, instead of merely reflecting inflation, capture the effect of relative changes in prices and in the composition of output. They also better reflect cyclical fluctuations in the economy.

SOURCE: U.S. Department of Transportation, Research and Innovative Technology Administration, Bureau of Transportation Statistics, based on data from U.S. Department of Commerce, Bureau of Economic Analysis, National Economic Accounts, National Incomes and Products Account, www.bea.gov/national/nipaweb/index.asp as of Mar. 14, 2009.

FIGURE 3

Quarter-to-Quarter Percent Change in Real Gross Domestic Product: 2007–2008
(Percent)

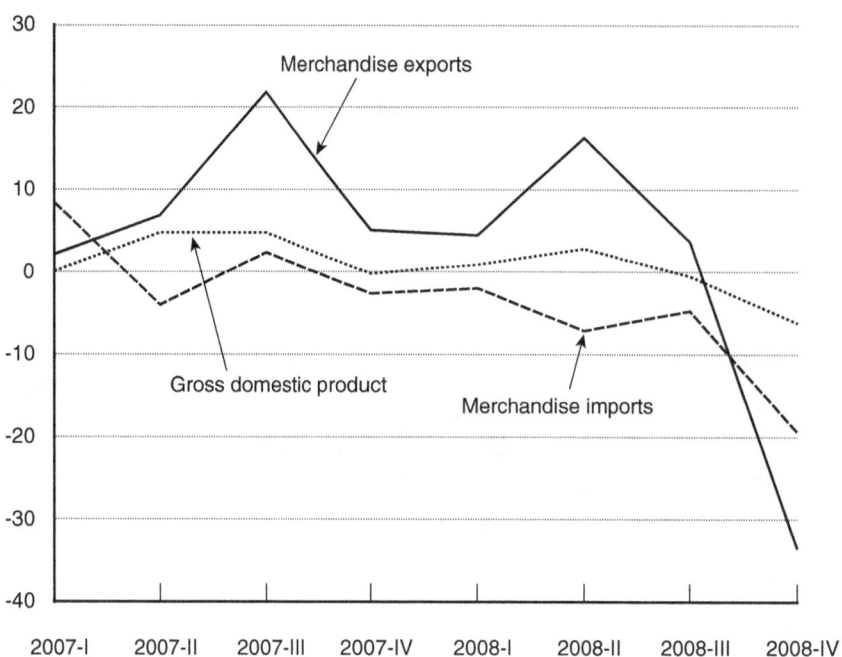

NOTE: Real GDP growth is measured at seasonally adjusted annual rates based on chained 2000 dollars.

SOURCE: U.S. Department of Transportation, Research and Innovative Technology Administration, Bureau of Transportation Statistics, based on data from U.S. Department of Commerce, Bureau of Economic Analysis, National Economic Accounts, National Incomes and Products Account, www.bea.gov/national/nipaweb/index.asp as of Mar. 14, 2009.

product (GDP)—the output of goods and services produced by labor and property located in the United States—decreased at an annual rate of 6 percent in the fourth quarter of 2008 (i.e., from the third quarter to the fourth quarter). In the third quarter, real GDP decreased 0.5 percent (USDOC BEA 2009). The slowdown in real GDP primarily reflected a sharp decline in personal consumption expenditure, the downturn in exports and imports, and a decline in state and local government spending.

Declines in economic activity and drops in exports and imports result in reduced demand for freight transportation services by all modes of transportation. However, because the majority of U.S. overseas merchandise trade (over 66 percent by value and 99 percent by weight) moves by ocean vessel (USDOC CB 2009), the nation's container ports felt the crunch immediately, but the effects were not limited to the seaports.[1]

[1] As used here, overseas trade excludes U.S. merchandise trade with Canada and Mexico.

EFFECTS OF DROP IN CONTAINER THROUGHPUT

The consequences of the 2008 decline in container throughput at the nation's seaports reached beyond marine ports and terminals, affecting containership fleet capacity, railroads and commercial trucks that service the seaports, and the inland warehouses and distribution centers that provide logistical support for the entire multimodal freight supply chain. First, because of the decline in global demand for containership services, the estimated number of container vessels idled at seaports worldwide soared by March 2009 to a record high of more than 450 ships with a carrying capacity of 1.4 million TEUs (AXS-Alphaliner 2009). These idle container vessels accounted for approximately 11 percent of the world containership fleet. The capacity of idle container vessels worldwide nearly tripled from the beginning of 2008, when it was estimated to be about 210 ships and 550,000 TEUs.

Second, with the overall decline in containerized exports and imports, the number of intermodal[2] shipping containers and truck trailers transported nationwide on railcars by the nation's Class I railroads[3] in 2008 was 11.5 million units, down 4 percent from 12 million in 2007 and from a record high of 12.3 million in 2006. About 60 percent of rail intermodal traffic consists of merchandise imports and exports (AAR 2009). In 2008, the number of international intermodal containers moved by rail from the seaports totaled 7.8 million, a decrease of 7 percent from 2007 (Intermodal Association of North America 2008). The imports arrive on ocean vessels and are long-hauled by railcars to destinations across the county, and the exports originate all across the nation and are headed for destinations around the world.

In one example of the severity of the declines, the leading Class I railroad for handling intermodal shipments from west coast ports, Union Pacific (UP), reported that the major economic downturn during the fourth quarter of 2008 compounded already declining intermodal volumes experienced earlier in the year and resulted in fewer intermodal shipments (Union Pacific Corp. 2009). UP's intermodal traffic from west coast intermodal terminals was 1.5 million container units in 2008, down 7 percent from 1.6 million units in 2007. In particular, at the Intermodal Container Transfer Facility in Los Angeles, UP's intermodal traffic dropped 13 percent during the same period.

There were similar declines in trucking services in the second half of 2008, resulting in record lows for overall freight trucking activity. In December 2008, according to the American Trucking Association (ATA),

trucking activity nationwide was down 13 percent from December 2007. Trucking services declined for 6 consecutive months, from June through December 2008 (ATA 2009).

Nationwide freight activity for all modes, measured by the Freight Transportation Services Index (TSI), declined 3.0 percent in 2008. According to the TSI, this decline was the third consecutive annual decline and the largest since 2000 (USDOT RITA BTS 2009). The freight TSI measures changes in the output of services provided by the for-hire freight transportation industries and consists of data from for-hire trucking, rail, inland waterways, pipelines, and air freight.

Third, the slowdown of economic activity within the United States, the reduction in consumer spending on foreign goods, and the decline in demand for freight transportation services resulted in excess inventory for certain imported products moved by ocean vessels, especially foreign automobiles. By March 2009, the parking lots of the nation's top auto ports had thousands of new car imports that could not be moved out. Auto dealers could not take delivery of them because of the drop in consumer demand and the lack of bank credit to finance their inventories (Leach 2009). The Port of Baltimore, the top auto-handling port in the United States, had about 57,000 new cars at its terminals and the port had to store some at the nearby Baltimore-Washington International Marshall Airport (Dennis 2009). Storage of imported autos at U.S. seaports further reduces demand for train and truck services to transport them to dealerships, dampens the market for third-party logistics services, decreases overseas car manufacturing, and ultimately increases the number of ocean vessels that are idled.

Globally, 1 maritime container in every 10 is bound to or originates in the United States.

TRENDS IN CONTAINER THROUGHPUT

Despite the 2008 decline in the nation's economic activity and international merchandise exports and imports, the United States remains the world's largest trading

---

[2] As used in this report, the term "intermodal" refers to the traditional rail and truck combination only. This involves using rail for the long-haul portion of the shipment and trucks for the shorter distances at both ends of the shipment. The term also could be used to describe shipments transported by multiple modes, including ocean vessels.

[3] Class I railroads are line-haul freight railroads with 2008 operating revenues exceeding $360 million.

TABLE 2
U.S. v. World Maritime Container Traffic and Gross Domestic Product: 1995–2008

	Container traffic (total TEUs loaded and empty)				Gross Domestic Product (current U.S. dollars)			
	World (millions)	United States (millions)	U.S. share of world total (percent)	U.S. rank	World GDP (billions)	United States (billions)	U.S. share of World GDP (percent)	U.S. rank
1995	137.2	22.3	16.3	1	29,391	7,398	25.2	1
1996	150.8	22.6	15.0	1	30,080	7,817	26.0	1
1997	160.7	24.5	15.3	1	29,928	8,304	27.7	1
1998	169.6	26.2	15.4	2	29,682	8,747	29.5	1
1999	184.6	28.0	15.2	2	30,786	9,268	30.1	1
2000	233.5	30.4	13.0	2	31,650	9,817	31.0	1
2001	245.1	30.7	12.5	2	31,456	10,128	32.2	1
2002	269.5	32.7	12.1	2	32,714	10,470	32.0	1
2003	307.4	36.3	11.8	2	36,751	10,961	29.8	1
2004	300.8	38.7	12.9	2	41,258	11,686	28.3	1
2005	306.0	42.0	13.7	2	44,455	12,422	27.9	1
2006	426.4	44.4	10.4	2	48,665	13,178	27.1	1
2007	436.6	45.0	10.3	2	54,585	13,808	25.3	1
2008	387.1	38.0	9.8	2	60,863[a]	14,265	23.4	1
Percent change, 1995-2008	182.1	70.1						
Average annual rate (percent), 1995-2008	8.3	4.2						

[a] World 2008 GDP is an estimate that includes projections by the International Monetary Fund for some countries.

KEY: TEUs = twenty-foot equivalent units. One 20-foot container equals one TEU, and one 40-foot container equals two TEUs.

SOURCES: TEUs, world estimates, 1995–1999: *Containerisation International Yearbook* (London: Informa Group, Inc., 1997–2001); 2000–2008: U.S. Department of Transportation, Maritime Administration, based on Containerisation International Online, www.ci-online.co.uk as of Mar. 30, 2009. TEUs, U.S. estimates, 1995–2007: American Association of Port Authorities, Industry Statistics; 1995–2007, www.aapa-ports.org/Industry as of Apr. 20, 2009; 2008: Containerisation International Online, www.ci-online.co.uk as of Apr. 20, 2009. GDP: World estimates from International Monetary Fund, World Economic Outlook Database, www.imf.org/external/pubs/ft/weo/2009/01/weodata/index.aspx as of Apr. 20, 2009; U.S. estimates from U.S. Department of Commerce, Bureau of Economic Analysis, www.bea.gov/national as of Mar. 30, 2009.

nation with the world's biggest economy. Today, 1 container in every 10 carrying global trade is bound for or originates in the United States, accounting for 10 percent of worldwide container traffic. In 2008, world maritime container traffic (loaded and empty) was estimated at over 387 million TEUs, down from 437 million TEUs transported in 2007 (table 2).

Between 1995 and 2008, world container traffic more than tripled in volume from 137 million TEUs to 387 million TEUs, growing at an average annual rate of about 8 percent (table 2). This continued long-term growth in maritime container freight reflects sustained U.S. and global economic activity. During this same period, U.S. total container traffic more than doubled in volume from 22 million TEUs in 1995 to an estimated 45 million in 2007,

falling to about 38 million in 2008. From 1995 to 2008, U.S. total TEUs rose at an average annual rate of 4.2 percent. The primary factors underlying the long-term growth in U.S. maritime container traffic are the proportion of merchandise trade transported in containers; rising trade with Asia-Pacific trading partners, particularly China; and the increasing importance of merchandise trade to U.S economic activity. Looking ahead, the volume of containers that U.S. seaports handle in the coming years will mainly be determined by how much the United States continues to rely on imported manufactured goods, which countries it trades with most, and what kinds of products it imports rather than produces domestically. Rising demand for foreign manufactured products would mean super-sized container vessels would carry such products to the nation's seaports, enabling continued growth in containerization.[4]

The United States ranked second in container traffic in 2007, a position it has held since China took over the number one position in 1998. Nonetheless, the United States remains the leading trading nation, accounting for 11 percent of total world merchandise trade in 2007 (figure 4). U.S. total imports ranked first, accounting for over 14 percent of the global imports in 2007. U.S. total exports accounted for 8 percent of global exports, behind Germany, the leading exporter (WTO 2008). The United States also remained the world's largest economy, accounting for 23 percent of World GDP in 2008, down slightly from 25 percent in 1995 (table 2).

---

[4] Containerization is a form of transportation in which the size and shape of freight is standardized through the use of containers to allow fast mechanical handling of cargo at seaports. It differs sharply from the labor-intensive and time-consuming break-bulk method of handling cargo of varying sizes and shapes.

From 1995 to 2008, the volume of containerized cargo moving through U.S. seaports grew at a faster rate, 6 percent, than U.S. real GDP growth, 3 percent (figure 5). During most of the 1990s, strong growth of the U.S. economy, rising household wealth and income in the United States, and steady consumer demand at home spurred U.S. international goods trade, which resulted in greater demands for containerized freight transportation services.

A comparison of the year-on-year percent change between U.S.-loaded container TEUs and real GDP shows a correlation between the container maritime industry trends and general economic conditions (figure 6). This comparison shows the effect that economic cycles have on the U.S. container trade, as evidenced by the declines in TEUs during the 2001 and 2008 recessions. As figure 6 shows, the container trade trend is more volatile than the GDP trend. However, assuming that the strong cyclical relationship continues, when the U.S. economy recovers and the volume of merchandise imports and ex-

U.S. container traffic doubled over the past decade, and the growth trend is expected to continue.

FIGURE 4
World's Top Merchandise Trade Countries: 2007
(Percent)

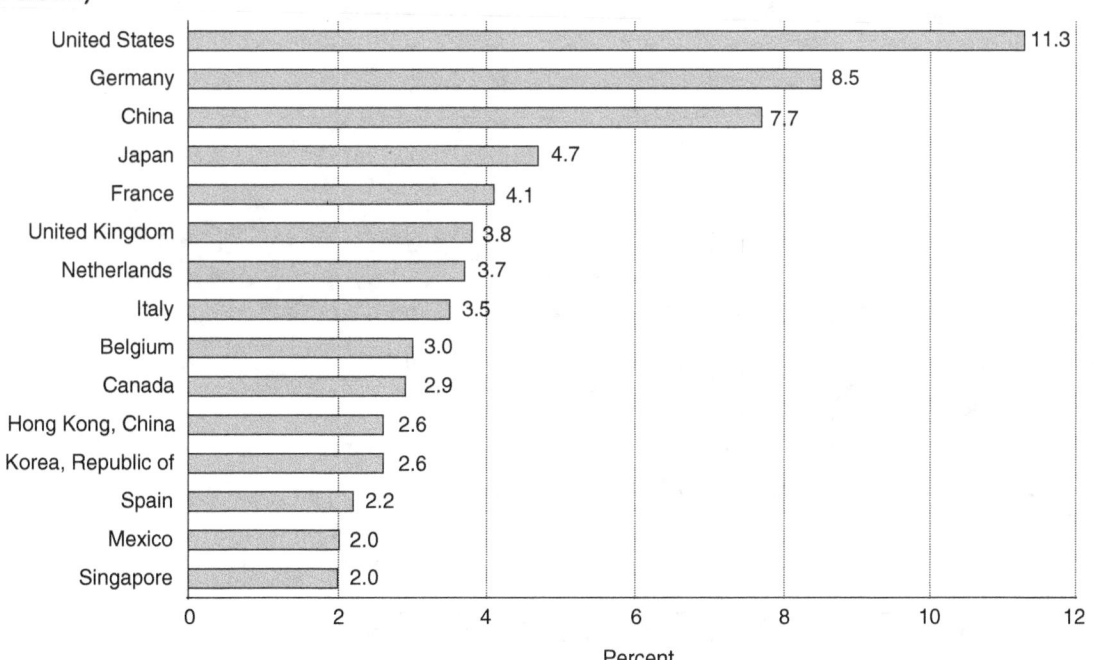

Country	Percent
United States	11.3
Germany	8.5
China	7.7
Japan	4.7
France	4.1
United Kingdom	3.8
Netherlands	3.7
Italy	3.5
Belgium	3.0
Canada	2.9
Hong Kong, China	2.6
Korea, Republic of	2.6
Spain	2.2
Mexico	2.0
Singapore	2.0

SOURCE: U.S. Department of Transportation, Research and Innovative Technology Administration, Bureau of Transportation Statistics, based on data from World Trade Organization, *2008 Trade Report.*

FIGURE 5

Growth in U.S. Container Trade, Overall Freight, and Real GDP: 1995–2008
(Index 2000 = 100)

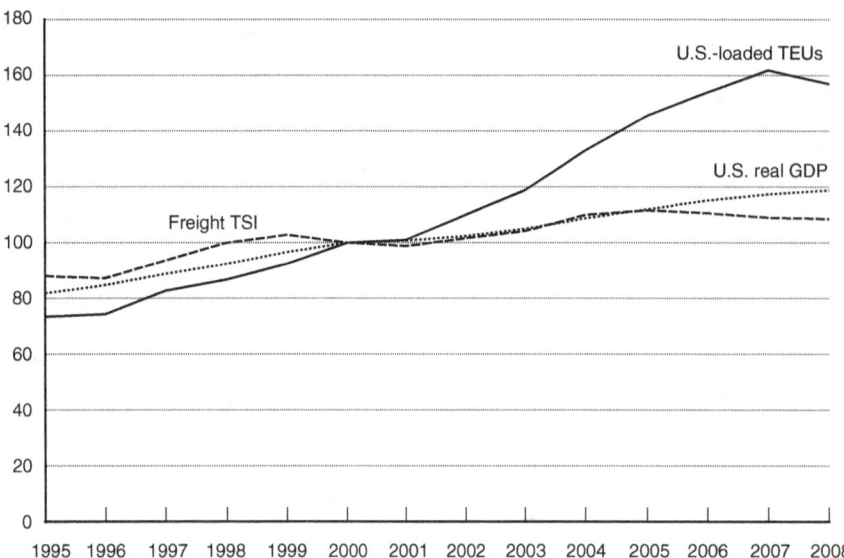

NOTE: Real GDP growth is measured at seasonally adjusted annual rates based on chained 2000 dollars. TSI figures are annualized estimates based on the monthly published estimates. TEUs = twenty-foot equivalent units.

SOURCE: U.S. Department of Transportation, Research and Innovative Technology Administration, Bureau of Transportation Statistics, based on data from U.S. Department of Commerce, Bureau of Economic Analysis, National Economic Accounts, National Incomes and Products Account, www.bea.gov/national/nipaweb/index.asp as of Mar. 14, 2009. TEU data based on data from U.S. Department of Transportation, Maritime Administration, which are drawn from *The Journal of Commerce*, Port Import Export Reporting Service (PIERS). Freight TSI data based on monthly freight TSI estimates from U.S. Department of Transportation, Research and Innovative Technology Administration, Bureau of Transportation Statistics, monthly TSI press releases at www.bts.gov.

FIGURE 6

Year-on-Year Percent Change in U.S. Container Trade and Real GDP: 1995–2008
(Percent)

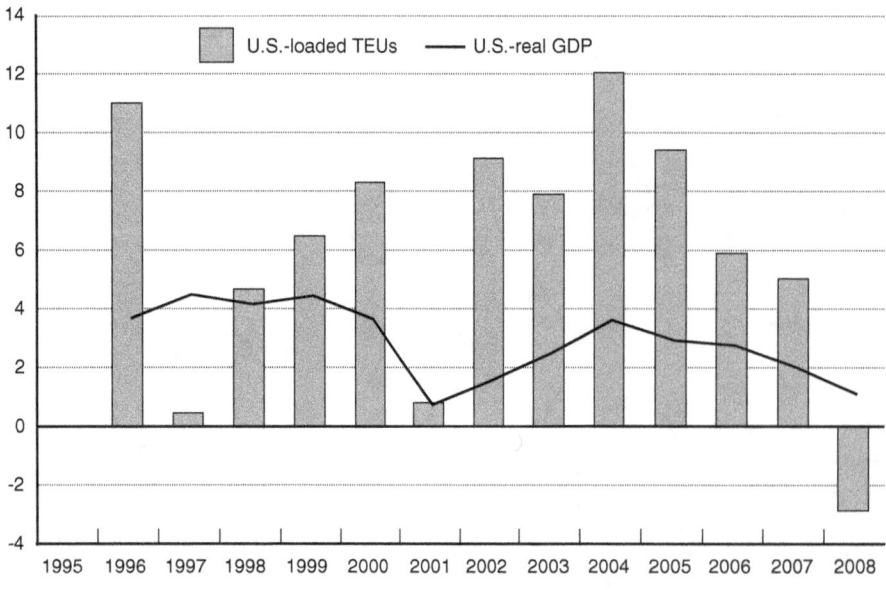

NOTE: Real GDP growth is measured at seasonally adjusted annual rates based on chained 2000 dollars.

SOURCE: U.S. Department of Transportation, Research and Innovative Technology Administration, Bureau of Transportation Statistics, based on data from Department of Commerce, Bureau of Economic Analysis, National Economic Accounts, National Incomes and Products Account, www.bea.gov/national/nipaweb/index.asp as of Mar. 14, 2009. TEU data based on data from U.S. Department of Transportation, Maritime Administration, which are drawn from *The Journal of Commerce*, Port Import Export Reporting Service (PIERS).

A broad challenge facing the U.S. maritime industry is the repositioning of empty containers after they have been emptied of the goods they transported to the United States. During the past 20 years, as merchandise trade between the United States and its trading partners—particularly Asia-Pacific Rim countries—mushroomed and the trade imbalance grew, the number of empty containers idling in the United States increased. In general, the larger the trade imbalance, the greater the need to reposition empty containers for shippers to use for exports.

Although containers are designed to be reused (with new cargo loaded for a new location soon after the original cargo is off-loaded), in many cases the cost of transporting an empty container to a place where it can be reloaded is higher than the container is worth, particularly when empty containers must be transported from inland locations to U.S. shippers or overseas.

In 1997, the difference between TEUs of U.S. containerized imports and exports was about 715,000. By 2006, the difference had reached a record high of nearly 10 million TEUs. In 2008, it was about 6 million TEUs. These large numbers illustrate the magnitude of the challenge of handling idle containers.

Empty containers are stored near seaports and inland intermodal transfer locations. Los Angeles, Long Beach, and New York/New Jersey are the three largest port markets where leasing companies and shipping lines store empty containers, and Chicago, Dallas, and Memphis are notable storage locations for empty containers inland (Mongelluzzo 2008). In 2008, the nation's top container port, the Port of Los Angeles, handled about 1.9 million TEUs of empty export containers, accounting for 51 percent of the total outbound export TEUs for the port.

ports rebounds, then U.S. container seaports are likely to see a resurgence of container throughput at their terminals.

GATEWAYS FOR INBOUND AND OUTBOUND TRAFFIC

While America's container seaports serve as gateways for both merchandise imports and exports, overall they handle more TEUs of imports than exports. In 2008, the U.S. deficit in maritime container traffic—the gap between exports and imports—narrowed to 6 million TEUs as maritime container imports fell 8 percent and exports grew 6 percent (figure 7). This marked the second year in a row that the deficit fell following record high imports in 2006. In 2007 and 2008, although the United States exported less abroad than it imported, imports declined steeply because of the

economic slowdown at home. Exports grew at a modest pace.

Before 1998, the deficit of U.S. international container traffic was less than 1 million TEUs per year, but by 2008, this gap had significantly widened, with imports accounting for a larger share of the total container traffic (figure 7). In 2008, maritime container imports passing through U.S. seaports accounted for 61 percent of total container traffic, a sizeable increase from 51 percent in 1995. However, container exports handled by the ports seem to be rebounding, reaching 39 percent of total container traffic in 2008, an increase from a low of 33 percent in 2005. A likely factor for the surge in exports during 2007 and 2008 is the fall of the U.S. dollar relative to the European euro and other currencies. During this period, as the dollar fell against the euro, American goods became more affordable overseas. This contributed to the rise in maritime container exports. A stronger dollar provides Americans with greater purchasing power and results in more goods being imported, while a weaker dollar leads to foreign buyers purchasing more U.S. products.[5]

Figure 8 shows the location of the nation's top 25 maritime container ports for U.S. international containerized exports and imports in 2008. The top three container port gateways were Los Angeles, Long Beach, and New York/New Jersey. The containerized exports and imports handled by these leading ports serve the international trade needs of every state, both coastal states with seaports as well as landlocked states that depend on seaports for their merchandise trade export and imports. The containerized cargo arrives and leaves the seaports either by rail or truck as single modes or by intermodal truck-rail combination.

Overall U.S. international maritime container traffic more than doubled between 1995 and 2008 (figure 9). In 2008, about 28 million TEUs of U.S. international oceanborne trade moved through U.S. container ports, up from 13 million in 1995 (JOC PIERS 2009b). As the rebound after the low year

---

[5] Because the merchandise trade deficit is more complicated than simple changes in relative prices, a fall in the U.S. dollar is not always effective in closing the gap between exports and imports. Domestic recessions are often more effective in cutting demand for imports and therefore reducing the trade balance.

FIGURE 7
U.S. International Maritime Container Traffic: 1995-2008
(Millions of TEUs)

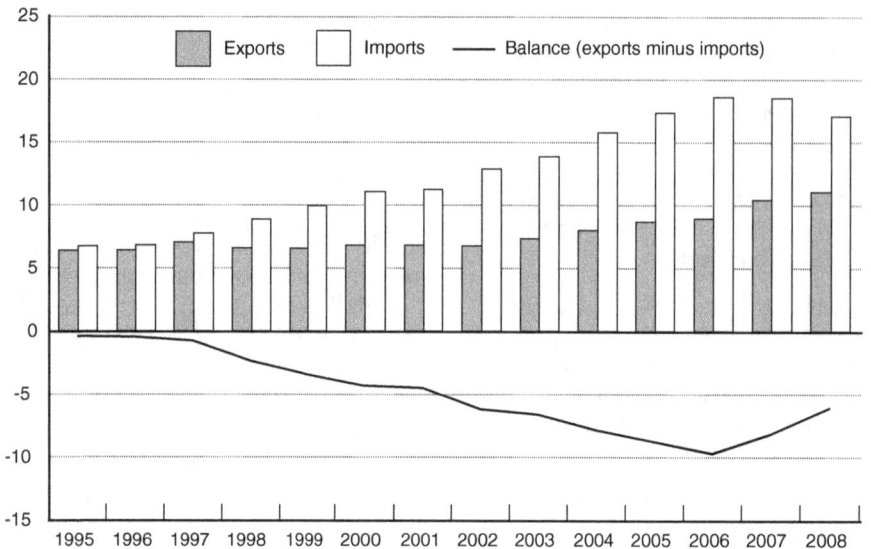

SOURCES: 1995–2004: U.S. Department of Transportation, Research and Innovative Technology Administration, Bureau of Transportation Statistics, based on data from U.S. Department of Transportation, Maritime Administration, which are drawn from *The Journal of Commerce*, Port Import Export Reporting Service (PIERS). 2005–2007: Data from the U.S. Department of Transportation, Maritime Administration, www.marad.dot.gov/data_statistics 2008: Estimate based on PIERS Trade Horizon estimate of annual percentage growth from 2007, reported at www.joc.com as of Mar. 19, 2009.

FIGURE 8
Top 25 Container Ports for U.S. International Maritime Freight: 2008
(Thousands of TEUs)

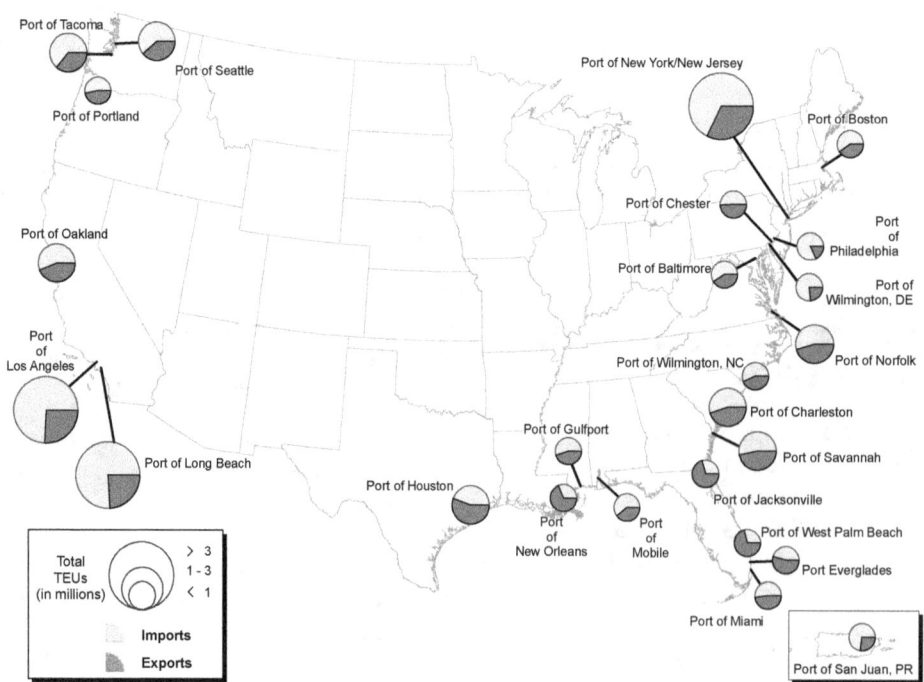

KEY: TEUs = twenty-foot equivalent units. One 20-foot container equals one TEU, and one 40-foot container equals two TEUs.

NOTE: The data in this figure include only loaded containers in U.S. international maritime activity and cover U.S. imports, exports, and transshipments. Therefore, the trade levels will be greater than those reported from U.S. international trade statistics, which exclude transshipments. The data also exclude military shipments.

SOURCE: U.S. Department of Transportation, Research and Innovative Technology Administration, Bureau of Transportation Statistics, based on data from U.S. Department of Transportation, Maritime Administration, which are drawn from *The Journal of Commerce*, Port Import Export Reporting Service (PIERS), available at www.marad.dot.gov as of Mar. 30, 2009.

in 2001 suggests, long-term growth is likely to resume after the U.S. and global economies recover from the current worldwide economic downturn.

In 2008, U.S. container ports handled a daily average of 77,000 TEUs, up from 37,000 TEUs per day in 1995. This large number of containers moving through the nation's seaports highlights the significance of container traffic and its potential impacts on the economy, local communities, national security, and the natural environment. It also underscores the challenges of handling this cargo efficiently, alleviating highway congestion around the seaports, improving landside access to ports, and removing freight bottlenecks at intermodal transfer locations where trucks and railroads connect to marine terminals.

A major factor affecting landside access to U.S. container ports is the continuing growth of containerization. Growth in containerization is directly related to the provision of adequate intermodal capacity to handle the associated increase in the level of landside traffic. For example, on a typical day in 2008, container throughput for the New York/New Jersey port, the nation's third largest container port, was 5,265,053 TEUs (PANYNJ 2009). Assuming a typical line-haul truck[6] carries an equivalent of two TEUs, this annual throughput translates into 2,632,526 one-way truck trips per year. This is equivalent to 10,125 truck trips each weekday resulting from containerized cargo. At approximately 40 feet per trailer, on a typical work day the trailers would stretch about 77 miles if lined up end to end.

---

[6] A line-haul truck is usually a tractor-trailer combination of three or more axles. A typical line-haul trailer is approximately 40 to 48 feet long and is permitted in most states to move a maximum of 80,000 pounds gross weight.

FIGURE 9
U.S. International Maritime Containerized Activity: 1995-2008
(Millions of loaded TEUs)

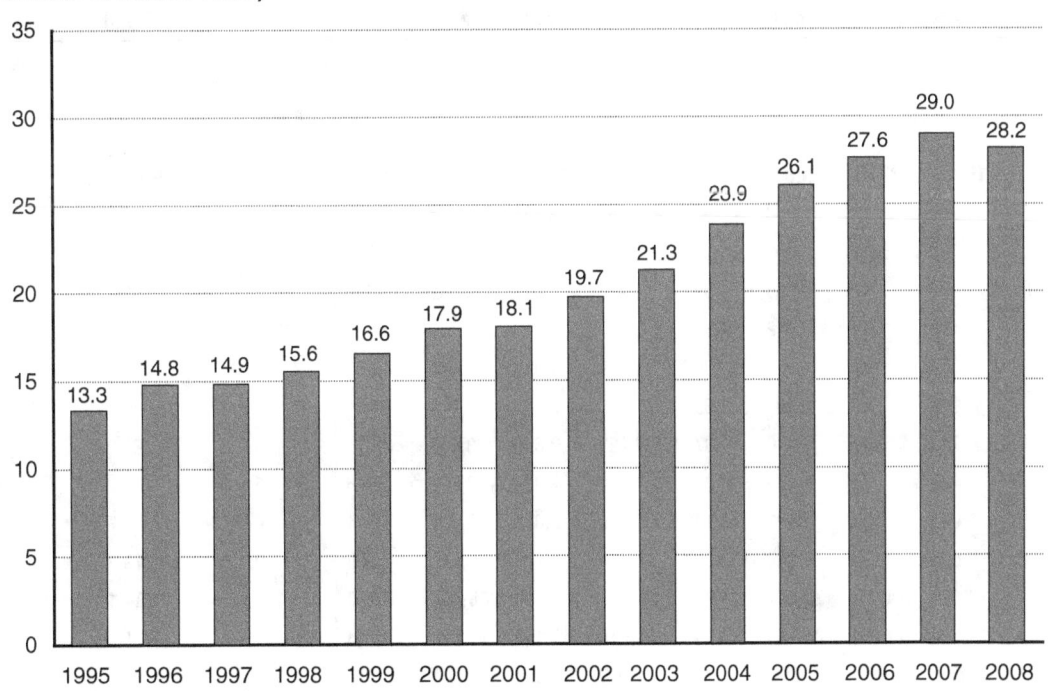

KEY: TEUs = twenty-foot equivalent units. One 20-foot container equals one TEU, and one 40-foot container equals two TEUs.

NOTES: Totals are for all container ports in all 50 states and Puerto Rico. The data in this figure include only loaded containers in U.S. international maritime activity and cover U.S. imports, exports, and transshipments.

SOURCE: 1995–2004: U.S. Department of Transportation, Research and Innovative Technology Administration, Bureau of Transportation Statistics, based on data from U.S. Department of Transportation, Maritime Administration, which are drawn from *The Journal of Commerce*, Port Import Export Reporting Service (PIERS). 2005–2007: Data from the U.S. Department of Transportation, Maritime Administration, www.marad.dot.gov/data_statistics 2008: Estimate based on PIERS Trade Horizon estimate of annual percentage growth from 2007, reported at www.joc.com as of Mar. 19, 2009.

PORT CONCENTRATION

The geographic distribution of container activity among U.S. seaports shows a greater concentration of vessel calls and cargo traffic in a few leading ports because of increased demand for larger, faster, and more specialized vessels. Today, maxi-Panamax superfreighter vessels are much longer than two football fields and can carry up to 12,500 TEUs.[7]

---

[7] These vessels are twice as large as the post-Panamax vessels. Post-Panamax vessels are too large to pass through the Panama Canal. They can carry up to 6,500 TEUs. They typically have widths exceeding 32.2 meters (105.6 feet). Recent designs of these vessels are able to carry more than 12,000 TEUs. The world's largest container vessel, Emma Maersk, commissioned in 2006, is officially listed as an 11,000 TEU ship, but its cargo capacity is estimated to range from 13,000 to 15,000 TEUs (http://about.maersk.com/en/Fleet/Pages/Fleet.aspx).

In 2008, the top 10 U.S. container ports accounted for 86 percent of containerized imports and exports (measured in TEUs), up from 78 percent in 1995. Five of the top 10 container ports in the United States are on the west coast, four are on the east coast, and one on the gulf coast (table 3).

From 1995 to 2008, Los Angeles and Long Beach grew the most in terms of absolute level of container traffic, reflecting increased U.S. trade with Pacific Rim[8] countries, particularly China, and the transportation of higher-value per ton Asian manufactured goods into the United States. New York followed closely, showing significant growth in U.S. trade with Europe. The ports of Savannah, Los Angeles, and Houston had the largest average annual growth rates (table 3). The growth rates for

---

[8] Pacific Rim refers to Australia, Cambodia, China, Indonesia, Japan, Malaysia, New Zealand, Philippines, Singapore, South Korea, Taiwan, Thailand, Vietnam, and various Pacific islands.

TABLE 3
Top 10 U.S. Maritime Container Ports by Loaded TEUs: 1995, 2000, 2007, and 2008

Port	Annual traffic (thousands)				Daily average				Trend		
	1995	2000	2007	2008	1995	2000	2007	2008	Percent change, 2007–2008	Percent change, 1995–2008	Average annual growth rate, 1995–2008 (percent)
Los Angeles, CA	1,849	3,228	5,740	5,671	5,066	8,843	15,727	15,537	-1.2	206.7	9.0
Long Beach, CA	2,137	3,204	4,995	4,612	5,855	8,777	13,685	12,635	-7.7	115.8	6.1
New York/New Jersey, NY/NJ	1,537	2,200	3,935	3,992	4,211	6,028	10,782	10,938	1.4	159.7	7.6
Savannah, GA	445	720	2,042	2,116	2,077	3,414	5,593	5,797	3.6	375.5	12.7
Norfolk, VA	647	850	1,573	1,592	1,219	1,973	4,310	4,360	1.2	146.0	7.2
Oakland, CA	919	989	1,451	1,395	2,518	2,709	3,976	3,821	-3.9	51.8	3.3
Charleston, SC	758	1,246	1,416	1,371	2,721	2,630	3,879	3,756	-3.2	80.8	4.7
Houston, TX	489	733	1,408	1,331	1,773	2,330	3,859	3,646	-5.5	172.2	8.0
Seattle, WA	993	960	1,151	1,129	1,340	2,009	3,152	3,094	-1.9	13.7	1.0
Tacoma, WA	604	647	1,289	1,083	1,654	1,773	3,533	2,966	-16.0	79.3	4.6
Total top 10 ports	10,378	14,777	25,001	24,291	28,432	40,486	68,495	66,550	-2.8	134.1	6.8
Total all ports[1]	13,328	17,938	28,969	28,190	36,515	49,144	79,368	77,234	-2.7	111.5	5.9
Top 10, percent of total	77.9	82.4	86.3	86.2	77.9	82.4	86.3	86.2			

[1] All container ports in all 50 states and Puerto Rico.

KEY: TEUs = twenty-foot equivalent units. One 20-foot container equals one TEU, and one 40-foot container equals two TEUs.

NOTE: The data in this table include only loaded containers in U.S. international maritime activity and cover U.S. imports, exports, and transshipments. Therefore, the trade levels will be greater than those reported from U.S. international trade statistics, which exclude transshipments. The data also exclude military shipments.

SOURCE: U.S. Department of Transportation, Research and Innovative Technology Administration, Bureau of Transportation Statistics, based on data from U.S. Department of Transportation, Maritime Administration, which are drawn from *The Journal of Commerce*, Port Import Export Reporting Service (PIERS) as of Mar. 20, 2009.

Savannah and Houston reflect the expansion in U.S. container trade with Latin American countries and changes in the location of freight logistics and distribution service centers.

Despite the national economic slowdown, container cargo handled by the Port of Savannah grew 4 percent in 2008 over 2007, the fastest growth among the leading container ports. Between 1995 and 2005, oceanborne containerized cargo handled there increased by 13 percent, making it the fastest growing port in the nation. This growth in Savannah's containerized traffic also underscores the increase in retail import distribution centers in the Savannah area—several national retailers have established large distribution centers there for handling the thousands of TEUs transiting the nation's seaports.

REGIONAL SHIFTS IN PORT MARKET SHARE

The increased use of oceanborne containers in transporting U.S. international trade continues to affect port operations and the distribution of total maritime trade among U.S. ports. Before the mid-1980s, when U.S. trade with Pacific Rim Asian countries was modest, east coast ports handled the majority of U.S. international maritime trade. As trade with Asia grew, the east coast ports' share of the value of trade declined and west coast ports' share increased (figure 10). Eventually, west coast ports surpassed east coast ports in maritime cargo handled, and this trend has continued to today. Also during this period, changes in industrial activity in the Midwest affected the volume and type of cargo moving through Great Lakes ports. For example, the relocation of final automobile assembly plants and companies that produce auto parts had an impact on manufacturing activities in the Midwest. With the emergence of automakers and parts producers in other parts of the United States, maritime cargo originating in the Midwest and cargo transport via the Great Lakes dwindled. Gulf of Mexico ports experienced a modest increase in their relative share as trade with Latin America grew.

Over half of U.S. containerized merchandise trade, measured in terms of TEUs, passes through west coast ports. In 2007, 55 percent of the container-

FIGURE 10
Coastal Port Region's Market Share of U.S. Containerized TEUs: 1980–2007

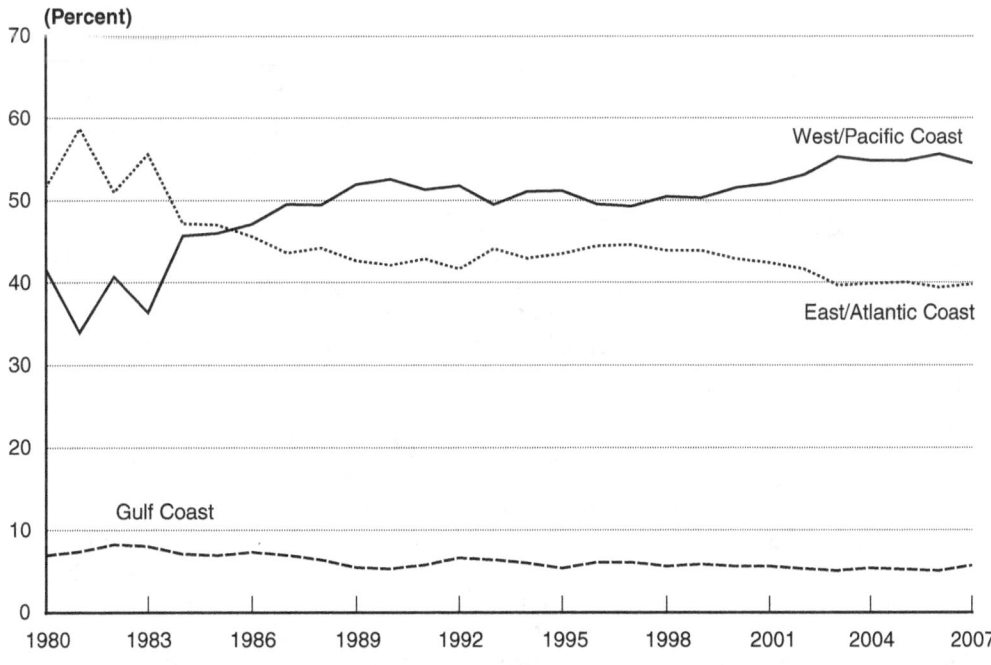

KEY: TEUs = twenty-foot equivalent units. One 20-foot container equals one TEU, and one 40-foot container equals two TEUs.

NOTES: Totals are for all container ports in all 50 states and Puerto Rico. The data in this figure include both loaded and unloaded containers in U.S. international maritime activity and cover U.S. imports, exports, and transshipments.

SOURCE: U.S. Department of Transportation, Research and Innovative Technology Administration, Bureau of Transportation Statistics, based on data from the American Association of Port Authorities, available at www.aapa.org as of Mar. 20, 2009.

FIGURE 11

Growth of U.S. Maritime Containerized Exports and Imports by Coastal Port Region: 1980-2007
(Index 1980 = 100)

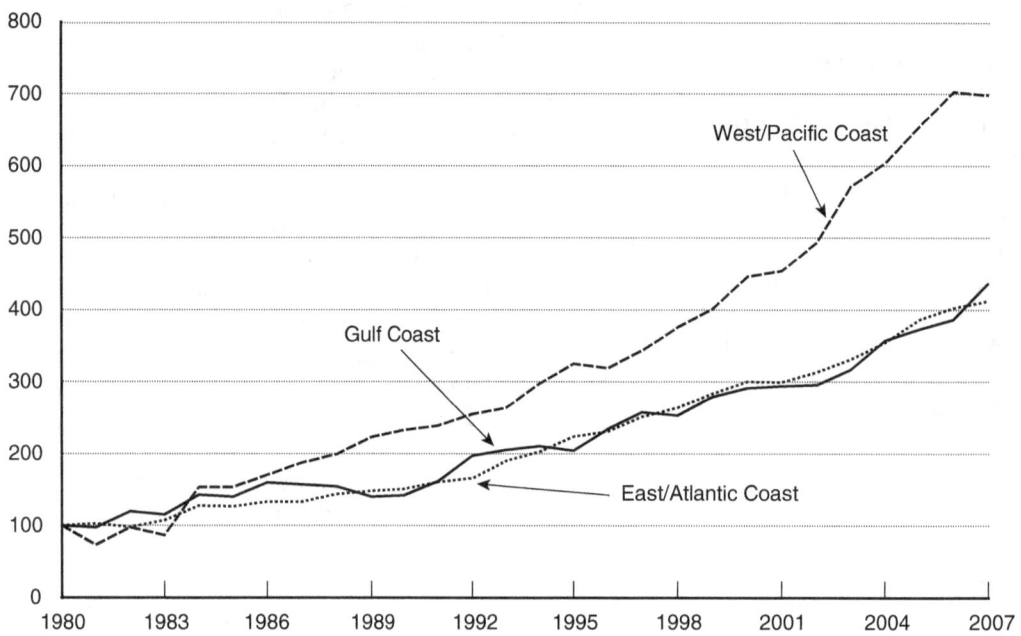

KEY: TEUs = twenty-foot equivalent units. One 20-foot container equals one TEU, and one 40-foot container equals two TEUs.

NOTES: Totals are for all container ports in all 50 states and Puerto Rico. The data in this figure include both loaded and unloaded containers in U.S. international maritime activity and cover U.S. imports, exports, and transshipments.

SOURCE: U.S. Department of Transportation, Research and Innovative Technology Administration, Bureau of Transportation Statistics, based on data from the American Association of Port Authorities, available at www.aapa.org as of Mar. 20, 2009.

ized imports and exports passed through these ports, up from 42 percent in 1980 (figure 10). West coast ports as a region grew the fastest during this period (figure 11).

Although west coast ports handled the most container trade, they also had a larger share of the oceanborne containerized trade deficit, in terms of export-import balance, than other regional ports. Today, west coast ports serve more as import gateways to the United States than as export gateways to the rest of the world. In contrast, east coast ports handle more exports than imports, despite the decline in their regional market share.

Container trade also affects the pattern of freight movement within the United States. Nearly all U.S. oceanborne container trade is transported throughout the country by either rail carriers, long-haul truck carriers, or local truck carriers. Some ports use short-sea shipping as an alternative to transport goods shorter distances.[9] The availability and

efficiency of intermodal transportation in moving these goods to and from any U.S. port increases shippers' choices of transportation modes and port facilities, allowing ports to effectively use their economies of scale to attract cargo from beyond their immediate region. The growth in U.S. containerized cargo shipping is placing pressure on the nation's transportation network and affects local traffic congestion and delays in the urban areas surrounding the major U.S. container ports. (See Spotlight 1 on landside access to the seaports.)

VESSEL CALLS AND CAPACITY

During the past two decades, the concentration of maritime container vessel calls at U.S. ports has shifted as the volume of containerized cargo handled by the ports has changed. In 2007, there were nearly 20,000 containership calls at U.S. seaports, accounting for 31 percent of the

[9] Short-sea shipping describes the movement of freight along coastal waterways (for example, from Long Beach to Portland

or from New York/New Jersey to Savannah). It includes the movement of containers and wet and dry bulk cargoes.

TABLE 4

Top 25 U.S. Container Ports by Containership Port Calls: 2007

Ranked by container capacity	Port/State	All vessel types		Containership		Containerships as percent of port's total vessels		Average vessel size per call (dwt)	
		Calls (total vessels)	Capacity (dwt, thousands)	Calls (total vessels)	Capacity (dwt, thousands)	Calls	Capacity	All vessel types	Containerships
1	Los Angeles/Long Beach, CA	5,492	335,898	3,058	169,562	55.7	50.5	61,161	55,449
2	New York/New Jersey, NY/NJ	4,968	232,426	2,549	127,359	51.3	54.8	46,785	49,964
3	San Francisco, CA	3,945	212,966	2,046	115,246	51.9	54.1	53,984	56,328
4	Savannah, GA	2,615	121,811	1,807	93,739	69.1	77.0	46,582	51,875
5	Virginia Ports, VA	2,775	137,548	1,940	91,138	69.9	66.3	49,567	46,979
6	Charleston, SC	2,160	96,571	1,589	76,622	73.6	79.3	44,709	48,220
7	Seattle, WA	1,042	59,936	666	39,485	63.9	65.9	57,520	59,287
8	Houston, TX	6,195	267,045	818	34,090	13.2	12.8	43,106	41,675
9	Tacoma, WA	1,241	62,621	621	33,262	50.0	53.1	50,460	53,562
10	Miami, FL	927	31,184	563	26,078	60.7	83.6	33,640	46,320
11	Port Everglades, FL	1,472	51,636	739	25,602	50.2	49.6	35,079	34,645
12	Baltimore, MD	1,833	63,052	427	17,793	23.3	28.2	34,398	41,671
13	Philadelphia, PA	3,148	191,814	499	15,594	15.9	8.1	60,932	31,250
14	Honolulu, HI	648	20,798	412	12,892	63.6	62.0	32,096	31,292
15	New Orleans, LA	4,884	239,972	281	12,189	5.8	5.1	49,134	43,379
16	San Juan, PR	1,045	23,484	498	11,464	47.7	48.8	22,473	23,020
17	Columbia River Ports, OR	2,578	99,772	154	7,473	6.0	7.5	38,701	48,529
18	Boston, MA	544	23,591	161	7,337	29.6	31.1	43,365	45,571
19	Jacksonville, FL	1,470	42,957	265	7,243	18.0	16.9	29,222	27,331
20	Dutch Harbor, AK	153	6,635	146	6,415	95.4	96.7	43,363	43,936
21	Wilmington, NC	562	22,322	102	5,477	18.1	24.5	39,718	53,698
22	Mobile, AL	885	47,279	50	2,110	5.6	4.5	53,423	42,195
23	Kodiak, AK	95	2,024	95	2,024	100.0	100.0	21,310	21,310
24	Anchorage, AK	184	4,265	94	2,007	51.1	47.1	23,179	21,356
25	Tampa, FL	800	28,652	36	1,416	4.5	4.9	35,815	39,328
	Total top 5 ports	19,795	1,040,649	11,400	597,044	57.6	57.4	52,571	52,372
	Total top 10 ports	31,360	1,558,006	15,657	806,582	49.9	51.8	49,681	51,516
	Total top 25 ports	51,661	2,426,260	19,616	943,620	38.0	38.9	46,965	48,105
	Total all U.S. ports[1]	63,804	3,295,980	19,863	947,862	31.1	28.8	51,658	47,720
	Top 5, percent of U.S. total	31.0	31.6	57.4	63.0				
	Top 10, percent of U.S. total	49.2	47.3	78.8	85.1				
	Top 25, percent of U.S. total	81.0	73.6	98.8	99.6				

KEY: dwt = deadweight tons.

NOTES: Data include oceangoing vessels 1,000 gross tons and above. Capacity equals dwt multiplied by calls. San Francisco includes Oakland, San Francisco, and other ports. Virginia ports include all Hampton Roads area ports (e.g., Norfolk, Newport News). Los Angeles and Long Beach are counted as one port in this table.

[1] All container ports in all 50 states and Puerto Rico. The data in this table include only loaded containers in U.S. international maritime activity and cover U.S. imports, exports, and transshipments. Therefore, the trade levels will be greater than those reported from U.S. international trade statistics, which exclude transshipments. The data also exclude military shipments.

SOURCE: U.S. Department of Transportation, Research and Innovative Technology Administration, Bureau of Transportation Statistics, based on data from U.S. Department of Transportation, Maritime Administration, which are drawn from the Lloyd's Maritime Intelligence Unit, Vessel Movement Data File, and are available at www.marad.dot.gov as of Mar. 20, 2009.

total oceangoing vessel calls made by all vessel types at U.S. ports.[10] The top five container ports handled over half (57 percent) of these container vessel calls and 63 percent of the container cargo capacity (table 4). Just 2 years before, in 2005, the top five ports handled 55 percent of the calls and 61 percent of the capacity.

Between 2002 and 2007, the number of vessel calls at U.S. container ports rose 16 percent, from about 17,100 to 19,800 calls. By contrast, total vessel calls grew by 13 percent, from 56,600 to 63,800 calls.

Measured by the average vessel size per call, U.S. maritime ports also handled larger container vessels than in the past. The average size (per call) of container vessels calling at U.S. ports was

---

[10] Of the remainder, 34 percent were by tankers, 17 percent by dry-bulk vessels, 10 percent by roll-on/roll-off ships, and 6 percent by general cargo ships.

nearly 48,000 deadweight tons (dwt) in 2007 (table 4). This is a significant increase from 38,000 dwt in 2000. Increases in vessel calls and containership capacity affect port operation, port productivity, and infrastructure requirements needed to accommodate the mega post-Panamax vessels. They also affect environmental considerations and community-impact issues. (See Spotlight 3 on ports and environmental concerns.)

RANKING OF U.S. PORTS AMONG WORLD'S TOP PORTS

In 2008, only 3 U.S. ports—Los Angeles, Long Beach, and New York/New Jersey—ranked among the world's top 20 container ports when measured by TEUs, placing 16th, 17th, and 20th, respectively (table 5). Since 2000, these 3 U.S. ports have dropped in the ranking of the world's top 20 ports as European and Southeast Asian ports handled

TABLE 5
Top 20 World Container Ports: 2000, 2007, and 2008
(Thousands of loaded and unloaded TEUs)

Rank in 2000	Rank in 2007	Rank in 2008	Port name	Country	2000	2007	2008	Percent change, 2000–2008	Percent change, 2007–2008	Average annual rate (percents), 2000–2008
2	1	1	Singapore	Singapore	17,040	27,932	29,918	76	7.1	7.3
6	2	2	Shanghai	China	5,613	26,150	27,980	398	7.0	22.2
1	3	3	Hong Kong	China	18,098	23,881	24,248	34	1.5	3.7
11	4	4	Shenzhen	China	3,994	21,099	21,414	436	1.5	23.4
3	5	5	Busan	South Korea	7,540	13,270	13,425	78	1.2	7.5
13	7	6	Dubai	United Arab Emirates	3,059	10,653	11,828	287	11.0	18.4
65	11	7	Ningbo	China	902	9,360	11,226	1,145	19.9	37.0
38	12	8	Guangzhou	China	1,430	9,200	11,001	669	19.6	29.1
5	6	9	Rotterdam	Netherlands	6,280	10,791	10,800	72	0.1	7.0
24	10	10	Qingdao	China	2,120	9,462	10,320	387	9.1	21.9
9	9	11	Hamburg	Germany	4,248	9,900	9,700	128	-2.0	10.9
4	8	12	Kaohsiung	Taiwan	7,426	10,257	9,677	30	-5.7	3.4
10	14	13	Antwerp	Belgium	4,082	8,177	8,664	112	6.0	9.9
32	17	14	Tianjin	China	1,708	7,103	8,500	398	19.7	22.2
12	16	15	Port Klang	Malaysia	3,207	7,120	7,970	149	11.9	12.1
7	13	16	Los Angeles	United States	4,879	8,355	7,850	61	-6.0	6.1
8	15	17	Long Beach	United States	4,601	7,312	6,488	41	-11.3	4.4
113	18	18	Tanjung Pelepas	Malaysia	418	5,500	5,600	1,239	1.8	38.3
17	20	19	Bremen/Bremerhaven	Germany	2,712	4,892	5,501	103	12.4	9.2
14	19	20	New York/New Jersey	United States	3,050	5,400	5,265	73	-2.5	7.1

KEY: TEUs = twenty-foot equivalent units. One 20-foot container equals one TEU, and one 40-foot container equals two TEUs.

SOURCES: 2000 and 2007: U.S. Department of Transportation, Research and Innovative Technology Administration, Bureau of Transportation Statistics, based on Maritime Administration, www.marad.dot.gov/data_statistics 2008: Containerisation International Online, www.ci-online.co.uk, as of March 17, 2009.

FIGURE 12

Top 20 World Container Ports: 2000 and 2008
(Millions of loaded and unloaded TEUs)

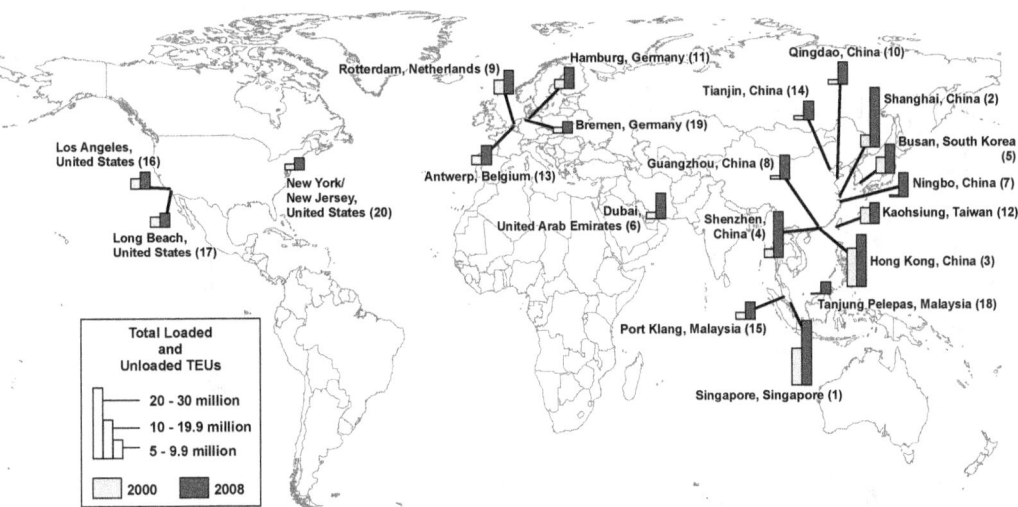

KEY: TEUs = twenty-foot equivalent units. One 20-foot container equals one TEU, and one 40-foot container equals two TEUs.

NOTE: Numbers in parenthesis are the 2008 port rankings.

SOURCES: 2000: U.S. Department of Transportation, Research and Innovative Technology Administration, Bureau of Transportation Statistics, based on U.S. Department of Transportation, Maritime Administration, www.marad.dot.gov/data_ statistics 2008: Containerization International Online, www.ci-online.co.uk as of Mar. 17, 2009.

more containerized cargo. During the same period, Chinese seaports became more dominant, and today 6 of the top 10 world ports are in China. Figure 12 shows the locations of the top 20 world container ports in 2008, the 2008 ranking by TEUs of cargo handled, and the cargo increases since 2000.

TRADING PARTNERS

While the United States exports and imports maritime goods from more than 175 countries, the vast majority of the trade is with relatively few countries. In 2007, nearly three-quarters (72 percent) of the container import TEUs were with 10 countries, and over half (55 percent) of the container export TEUs were with 10 countries. The top five overall U.S. containerized cargo trading partners in 2007 were all Asian countries: China (mainland),[11] Japan, Hong Kong (China), South Korea, and Taiwan. China (mainland) was the leading containerized merchandise trading partner, accounting for 47 percent of U.S. maritime import TEUs, up from 25

percent in 2000. China accounted for 18 percent of the export TEUs in 2007, down slightly from 2005 (figures 13 and 14).

Between 2000 and 2007, while China's share grew of total U.S. container trade, the other top five trading partners saw declines in their total maritime containerized cargo with the United States. Japan is now the second largest trading partner for U.S. oceanborne containerized exports, having been overtaken by China in 2003. In 2007, the U.S. maritime container imports from China alone were larger than those from more than 170 countries combined (i.e., those countries grouped into "other" (figure 13)).

U.S. imports and exports with major trading partners vary by types of goods, and this affects the types of vessels (for example, container, dry bulk, general cargo, or tanker), number of port calls, and the seaports the vessels use. For instance, while most U.S.-Canada maritime trade involves agricultural products, lumber, and petroleum products, most U.S.-Germany maritime trade involves manufactured products such as automobiles and machinery. In addition, U.S. maritime imports from Japan were valued at over $7,000 per ton, but U.S. exports to Japan were valued at $800 per ton,

---

[11] For the analysis in this report, U.S. merchandise trade with mainland China and Hong Kong are considered separate. As used here, China refers to mainland China.

FIGURE 13
Top 10 Trading Partners for U.S. Waterborne Containerized Imports: 2000, 2005, and 2007
(Percent)

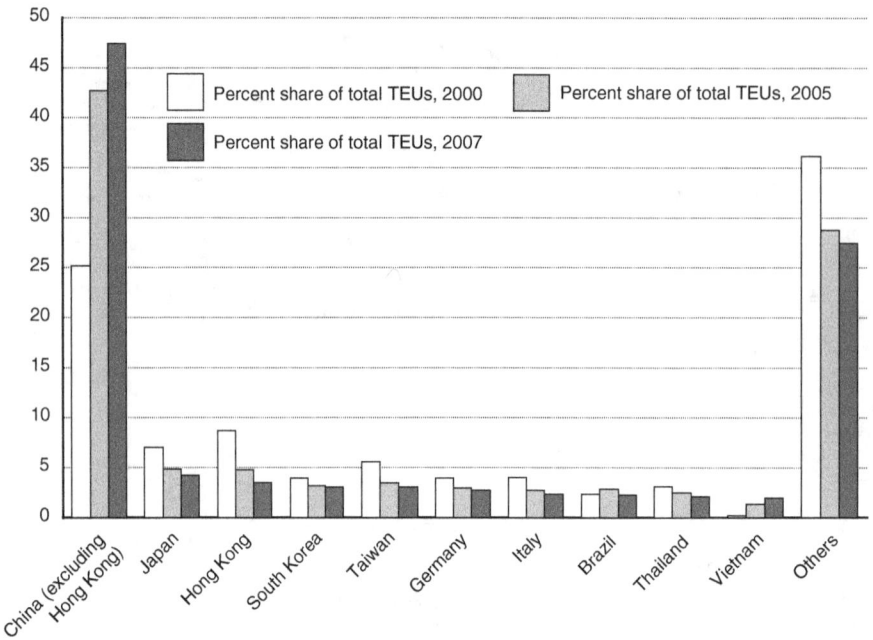

NOTE: For the analysis in this report, U.S. merchandise trade with mainland China and Hong Kong are considered separately. As used here, China refers to mainland China.

SOURCE: U.S. Department of Transportation, Research and Innovative Technology Administration, Bureau of Transportation Statistics, based on data from U.S. Department of Transportation, Maritime Administration, www.marad.dot.gov/data_statistics 2008 as of Apr. 20, 2009.

FIGURE 14
Top 10 Trading Partners for U.S. Waterborne Containerized Exports: 2000, 2005, and 2007
(Percent)

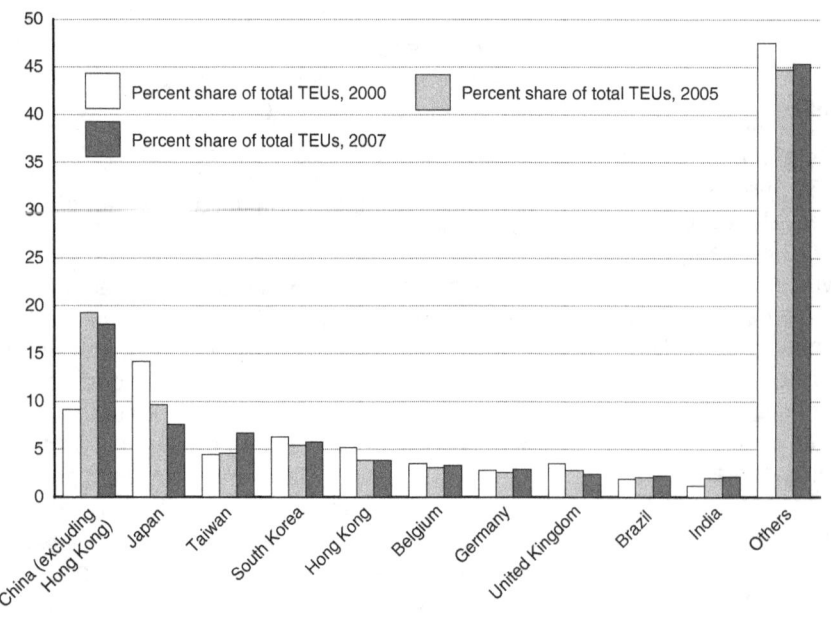

NOTE: For the analysis in this report, U.S. merchandise trade with mainland China and Hong Kong are considered separately. As used here, China refers to mainland China.

SOURCE: U.S. Department of Transportation, Research and Innovative Technology Administration, Bureau of Transportation Statistics, based on data from U.S. Department of Transportation, Maritime Administration, www.marad.dot.gov/data_statistics 2008 as of Apr. 20, 2009.

reflecting differences in the types of goods and the growth in high-value containerized imports to U.S. ports. Major U.S. maritime imports from Japan include passenger cars, car parts, and electronic equipment, and major U.S. maritime exports to Japan include agricultural products, industrial machinery, and chemicals.

ENTRIES OF OCEANBORNE CONTAINER UNITS

The container entries data from U.S. Customs and Border Protection (CBP) represented in this section and the next and in figures 15 and 16 are different from the TEU data presented earlier in the report. The CBP entries data count individual container units, while the TEU data refer to 20-foot equivalent units (that is, one 20-foot container equals one TEU, and one 40-foot container equals two TEUs). Because containers come in different lengths (for example, 20 feet, 40 feet, and 48 feet), the CBP figures on individual units differ from the TEU figures, which convert the tonnage of goods moved in the containers into TEUs.

The challenge of handling large volumes of containerized imports from U.S. trading partners can also be seen in the number of individual container entries processed by CBP. After a slight decline in the number of oceanborne containers entering the United States in the aftermath of the September 11, 2001, attacks, the nation's seaports again

began handling an increasing number of container units. In 2007, there were about 12 million ocean-borne container entries into the United States, down slightly from 2006 but still double those of 2000 (figure 15). Maritime container entries peak in the summer months, when imported merchandise trade is delivered for the fall and holiday seasons (figure 16).

CONTAINER ENTRIES BY ALL MODES FROM ALL COUNTRIES

On a typical day in 2007, more than 70,000 individual container units entered the United States by ocean vessel, truck, and rail. In 2000, the figure was about 50,000 units per day.

Overall, there were over 25 million container entries into the United States by all modes of transportation in 2007, up 38 percent from nearly 19 million in 2000. In addition to the more than 11 million oceanborne containers used to bring goods into the United States, over 14 million containers entered the nation by truck and rail from Canada and Mexico in 2007 (table 6). The large number of containers crossing by land border into the United States by surface modes reflects the importance of U.S. trade with two of our top three trading partners. From 2000 to 2007, the number of truck, rail, and maritime container units (loaded and un-loaded) crossing into the United States rose by 8 percent, 27 percent, and 94 percent, respectively.

Table 6
Container Entries into the United States from All Countries and by All Modes: 2000–2008
(Thousands of entries)

	Vessel containers full	Vessel containers empty	Truck containers full	Truck containers empty	Rail containers full	Rail containers empty	Overall total
2000	5,353	635	7,685	2,748	1,482	685	18,587
2005	10,933	481	8,850	2,603	1,794	875	25,536
2006	11,238	480	8,721	2,689	1,792	935	25,855
2007	11,038	578	8,428	2,791	1,748	1,005	25,588
2008	NA	NA	7,680	2,947	1,645	1,029	NA
Modal shares (percent)							
2000	28.8	3.4	41.3	14.8	8.0	3.7	100.0
2005	42.8	1.9	34.7	10.2	7.0	3.4	100.0
2006	43.5	1.9	33.7	10.4	6.9	3.6	100.0
2007	43.1	2.3	32.9	10.9	6.8	3.9	100.0
2008	NA	NA	NA	NA	NA	NA	NA

KEY: NA = Not available.

SOURCE: U.S. Department of Transportation, Research and Innovative Technology Administration, Bureau of Transportation Statistics, based on data from U.S. Department of Homeland Security, Customs and Border Protection, Mission Support Services, Operations Management Database.

FIGURE 15

Maritime Container Entries into the United States: 2000-2007

(Millions of container units of all sizes)

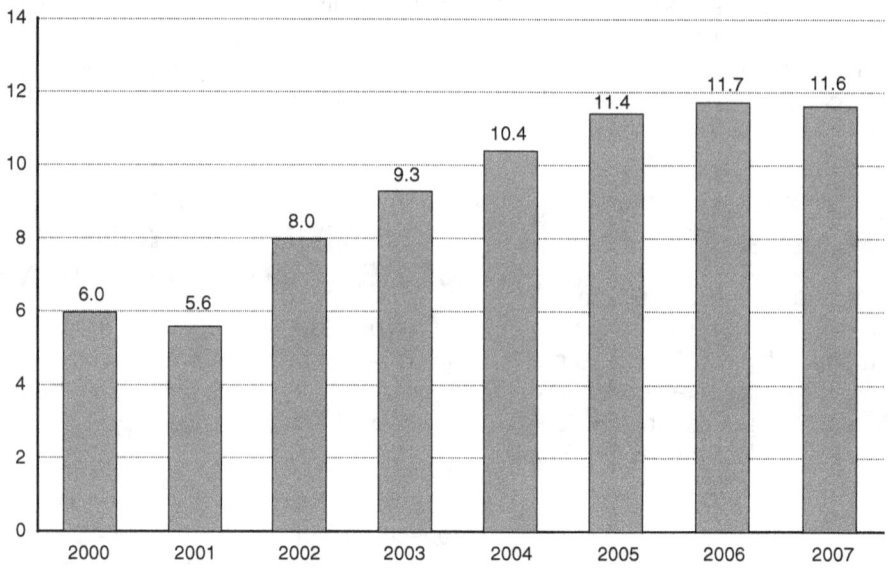

SOURCE: U.S. Department of Transportation, Research and Innovative Technology Administration, Bureau of Transportation Statistics, based on data from U.S. Department of Homeland Security, Customs and Border Protection, Mission Support Services, Operations Management Database.

FIGURE 16

Monthly Maritime Container Entries into the United States: 2006–2007

(Thousands of container units of all sizes)

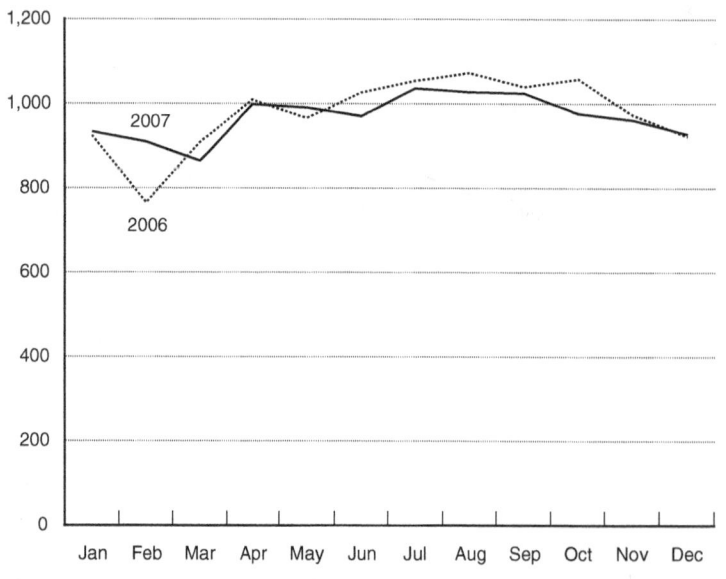

SOURCE: U.S. Department of Transportation, Research and Innovative Technology Administration, Bureau of Transportation Statistics, based on data from U.S. Department of Homeland Security, Customs and Border Protection, Mission Support Services, Operations Management Database.

SPOTLIGHT 1: LANDSIDE ACCESS TO SEAPORTS

While container traffic at U.S. ports has increased steadily for many years, landside access to ports has not kept pace. Improving the intermodal connections for freight moving through ports remains a daunting task. Many cities grew around their ports, and thus many ports are now surrounded by dense urban environments. New rights-of-way for rail or truck traffic leaving port facilities are not available, restricting rail or road expansion.

Containerization has dramatically reduced the time needed to load and unload a vessel, but it has also contributed to landside congestion at ports. As containerships continue to increase in size, the number of containers they bring at one time also increases, shifting congestion from the waterways to the rail and truck infrastructure that serve the ports (USDOT FHWA 2008). The practice of double-stacking containers on railcars has been constrained in some locations because of low bridge and tunnel clearances. New facilities are needed to better enable the transfer of containers from ships to railcars and trucks. Finding locations for these large facilities in busy port and urban areas, however, is a problem (National Surface Transportation Policy and Revenue Study Commission 2007). While containerized international trade is predicted to double between 2001 and 2020, container capacity at U.S. ports has not grown in proportion to that of U.S. trading partners. By 2010, the container port in Singapore alone will have more container capacity than all the U.S. container ports combined (USDOT MARAD 2005). As of 2005, congestion resulting from landside access challenges was estimated to cost as much as $200 billion, wasting 2.3 billion gallons of fuel and 3.7 billion man-hours annually (USDOT MARAD 2005).

This section briefly presents the components of the intermodal freight system that operates at U.S. ports and discusses efforts at improving landside access and intermodal connectivity.

Intermodal Infrastructure at U.S. Ports

Railroads

America's rail system consists of 162,000 miles of track that is privately owned and operated (AAR 2008). Following deregulation in 1980, the freight rail industry underwent years of downsizing, but it is now experiencing demand that is greater than capacity. Intermodal freight rail (the movement of containers or truck trailers from ports by rail) has increased substantially—from 3 million trailers and containers in 1980 to more than 12 million in 2007. Railroads have invested heavily in intermodal infrastructure to accommodate intermodal demand—for example, investing in intermodal freight cars, raising bridge and tunnel clearances to accommodate double-stacked containers, laying additional track, and implementing new communications systems (AAR 2008).

NHS Freight Connectors

Public roads that connect major intermodal freight terminals with the arterials and interstates of the National Highway System (NHS) are designated as NHS freight connectors. While these connectors are often short (often 2 miles long or less), they serve a vital purpose in America's economy. A 2000 study of NHS freight connectors found that connectors to ports had "twice the percent of mileage with pavement deficiencies when compared to non-Interstate NHS routes" (USDOT FHWA 2000).

The Marine Transportation System

The Marine Transportation System (MTS) consists of all of the intermodal components that are part of the maritime domain, including ships, ports, inland waterways, intermodal rail and truck, and MTS users (USDOT MARAD 2005). Although in recent years the demands placed on ports have been significant, some ports have had excess waterside capacity because problems with their landside access have discouraged use of them (NRC TRB 2003).

Congestion Mitigation and Access-Improvement Strategies

U.S. economic expansion and international trade are inextricably linked to the resolution of congestion and landside access challenges at U.S. ports. In recognition of this need, public and private MTS stakeholders have examined strategies for reducing landside congestion and improving access.

A comprehensive research project to find "low-cost and quickly implementable approaches" to reduce freight access and congestion challenges is currently under way through the National Cooperative Freight Research Program (NCFRP). The approaches reviewed for this study include radio frequency identification devices (RFID) on containers to allow operators to better position specific containers according to when they need to be transported, virtual container yards,[12] congestion pricing, inland ports, extended business hours, truck-only lanes, and on-dock rail access (GAO 2008a).

Traffic bottlenecks on the landside transportation system serving the nation's seaports affect seaports' performance and the efficient movement of goods in and out of the ports.

In 2005, the most recent year for which data on both port freight activity and landside traffic delay are available, the top seaports ranked by port vessel calls were the ports of Los Angeles and Long Beach (table 7). The Los Angeles-Long Beach metropolitan area was also the top ranked urban area in 2005 in terms of annual traffic delay per traveler, averaging about 72 hours of delay.

Growing traffic delays on the access routes serving the nation's largest seaports combined with the rising volumes of inbound and outbound cargo may result in increased congestion in the surrounding communities.

---

[12] Virtual container yards are Web-based platforms where users can match empty containers to container needs at the dock rather than returning them to the terminal.

TABLE 7

U.S. Maritime Port Activity and Landside Traffic Delay per Traveler in Surrounding Urban Area: 2007

Ranked by port calls by all vessel types	Port	Port calls and capacity by all vessel types		Overall maritime cargo tonnage (domestic and international)		Landside annual traffic delay per traveler in surrounding urban area (2005)[1]	
		Calls	Capacity (dwt, millions)	Total short tons (millions)	Rank by tonnage	Hours of delay	Rank
1	Houston, TX	6,195	267	216	2	56	7
2	Los Angeles/Long Beach, CA	5,492	336	151	4	72	1
3	New York, NY	4,968	232	157	3	46	16
4	New Orleans, LA	4,884	240	76	9	18	63
5	San Francisco Bay Area ports, CA[2]	3,945	213	48	17	60	2
6	Philadelphia/Delaware River ports, PA[3]	3,148	192	111	5	38	33
7	Virginia ports, VA[4]	2,775	138	56	15	30	42
8	Savannah, GA	2,615	122	36	23	NA	NA
9	Columbia River ports, OR[5]	2,578	100	56	14	38	33
10	Charleston, SC	2,160	97	23	33	31	40
11	Baltimore, MD	1,833	63	41	20	44	22
12	Port Everglades, FL	1,472	52	24	32	NA	NA
13	Jacksonville, FL	1,470	43	21	35	39	29
14	Port Arthur, TX	1,418	95	29	27	11	77
15	Tacoma, WA	1,241	63	27	29	45	19
16	Texas City, TX	1,200	70	57	13	56	7
17	Corpus Christi, TX	1,080	72	81	7	10	80
18	San Juan, PR	1,045	23	12	45	NA	NA
19	Seattle, WA	1,042	60	28	28	45	19
20	Miami, FL	927	31	7	56	50	11
21	Mobile, AL	885	47	64	10	NA	NA
22	Freeport, TX	806	40	30	26	NA	NA
23	Tampa, FL	800	29	47	18	NA	NA
24	Lake Charles, LA	796	56	64	11	NA	NA
25	Honolulu, HI	648	21	18	37	24	51

KEY: dwt = deadweight tons. NA = Not available in the Texas Transportation Institute 2007 Annual Urban Mobility Study.

1 The most recent year for which data on landside annual traffic delay are available is 2005. Annual delay per traveler equals extra travel time for peak-period travel during the year divided by the number of travelers who begin a trip during the peak period (6 to 9 a.m. and 4 to 7 p.m.). These peak-period travel times are compared wih times for free-flow speeds (60 mph on freeways and 35 mph on principal arterials).

2 San Francisco Bay Area ports: Oakland, Redwood City, Richmond, San Francisco, and Stockton.

3 Philadelphia/Delaware River ports: Philadelphia, Paulsboro, Marcus Hook, Camden-Gloucester, Chester, and Wilmington.

4 Virginia ports: Norfolk, Richmond, and Newport News.

5 Columbia River ports: Portland, Longview, Vancouver, and Kalama.

SOURCES: U.S. Department of Transportation, Research and Innovative Technology Administration, Bureau of Transportation Statistics, based on data from three sources. Port calls data: Maritime Administration, Ports Calls Data, at www.marad.dot.gov, as of Mar. 31, 2009. Cargo weight data: U.S. Army Corps of Engineers, Waterborne Commerce Statistics Center, at www.iwr.usace.army.mil/ndc/wcsc/wcsc.htm, as of Mar. 31, 2009. Traffic delay data: Texas Transportation Institute, 2007 Annual Urban Mobility Study, Table 1, available at mobility.tamu.edu/ums as of Mar. 30, 2009.

SPOTLIGHT 2: MARITIME SECURITY

Securing maritime cargo globally throughout the entire supply chain remains a security challenge for shipping lines, vessel owners, and shippers. In 2007 and 2008, the issue of piracy and hijacking of ocean vessels on the high seas became a major concern, particularly for vessels passing through the Gulf of Aden on the east coast of Africa. In 2008, more than 120 pirate attacks occurred in the Gulf of Aden (New York Times 2009). On April 8, 2009, a U.S.-flagged container vessel with 20 American sailors was hijacked by pirates off the coast of Somalia. The vessel's crew later regained control of the ship. The International Maritime Bureau estimates that between January and April 2009, there were 41 attempted pirate attacks and 6 hijackings in Gulf of Aden (ICC Commercial Crime Services 2009). Preventing such attacks in the vast open oceans is an enormous challenge for the international maritime community.

The security of U.S. ports and the goods that pass through them depends on numerous governmental actors, foreign and domestic, and private-sector entities. Following the terrorist attacks of September 11, 2001, attention to maritime trade security increased substantially. Legislation and related government strategies have proliferated, but significant concerns remain about the overall security of maritime trade.

Several long-term trends in maritime trade have made it more difficult for U.S. authorities to secure maritime cargo. In the second half of the 20th century, globalization transformed the nation's economy. The production of many goods moved to low-cost locations overseas, necessitating an increase in maritime trade. Containerization, the use of large aluminum or steel containers to ship freight, aided globalization by reducing the amount of time and labor needed to ship goods and by reducing cargo damage (OECD 2003). The trend toward just-in-time (JIT) production and inventory management, in which firms seek to cut costs and improve efficiencies through a build-to-order strategy that dramatically reduces their inventories, has provided many benefits to shippers, but it has also presented complex security challenges.[13]

Because containers make up the largest percentage of inbound maritime cargo traffic, they have been the focus of security efforts. Containers obscure cargo from plain sight. Because of the high volume of imported containers handled at U.S. seaports, it is a challenge to attempt to inspect every container without severely interrupting the flow of trade. Containers, and the items they transport, often take circuitous routes from origin to destination, not only passing port to port but traveling inland via rail or truck. An average container makes 17 stops between its origin and final destination. Tampering with containers—inserting illicit material—is not difficult at most points in the supply chain (Cohen 2006).

U.S. authorities have taken a multilayered approach that attempts to provide maritime freight security throughout the international supply chain. This section reviews the current maritime security system and the difficult challenges the United States faces in providing a completely secured maritime transportation system.

Post-9/11 Security Improvements

The September 11, 2001, terrorist attacks dramatically increased public-sector attention to maritime transportation system security. In fiscal year 2001, federal funding for port security was approximately $259 million. By fiscal year 2005, it had risen to $1.6 billion, a 700 percent increase (USDHS CBP 2006).

---

[13] JIT involves keeping materials on hand for only a few days or sometimes only a few hours of operation.

TABLE 8

Post-9/11 Legislation Relevant to Maritime Transportation System Security

Legislation	Purpose
Aviation and Transportation Security Act (2001)	Gave the federal government broad authority in transportation security for all modes.
Maritime Transportation Security Act (2002)	Required the U.S. Department of Homeland Security to create the National Maritime Security Plan. This plan outlines the coordinated action and incident-response plans between federal, state, and local governments to respond to security incidents involving maritime assets and infrastructure. The act also required, among other things, the establishment of transportation worker identification cards, maritime safety and security teams, port security grants, and enhancements to maritime intelligence and matters dealing with foreign ports and international cooperation.
Critical Infrastructure Information Act (2002)	Created the framework that allows private-sector entities and others to voluntarily submit information regarding critical infrastructure/key resources in their possession to the U.S. Department of Homeland Security, with the assurance that this information will not be publicly available.
The Intelligence Reform and Terrorism Prevention Act (2004)	Required the development of the National Strategy for Transportation Security. This strategy is a classified document, but it is known that this document provides the framework for the federal government, working with state, local, and tribal governments and private industry, to secure the national transportation system and to prepare to respond to terrorist threats or attacks to transportation infrastructure.
Security and Accountability for Every Port Act (2006)	Required the secretary of homeland security, in coordination with relevant federal, state, local, and tribal government authorities and the private sector and international community, to develop and implement a strategic plan to "enhance the security of the international supply chain."

SOURCE: U.S. Department of Homeland Security, Draft Strategy to Enhance International Supply Chain Security, July 2007.

Table 8 summarizes some of the significant maritime security legislation in the post- 9/11 period. The Maritime Transportation Security Act of 2002 (MTSA) and the Security and Accountability for Every Port Act of 2006 (SAFE Port Act) are among the most important pieces of legislation. Out of MTSA, the National Maritime Transportation Security Plan was created to provide a framework for deterrence of security incidents involving maritime transportation infrastructure and for response to any that may arise. This plan requires two levels of security planning at the local level, the Area Maritime Security Plans (AMSP) and the Vessel and Facility Security Plans (VSPs and FSPs, respectively). AMSPs are developed by the local U.S. Coast Guard sector commander/federal maritime security coordinator, with input from the area maritime security committees, which include government officials and other key stakeholders. Facility owners or vessel owners or operators create VSPs and FSPs. There are eight additional mode-specific security plans that are subsidiaries of the National Maritime Transportation Security Plan.

Under the SAFE Port Act, the Draft Strategy to Enhance International Supply Chain Security was produced in July 2007.[14] The U.S. Department of Homeland Security (USDHS) is the lead agency in implementing this strategy. It provides an overarching framework to facilitate the secure flow of international cargo, provides plans for specific segments of the international supply chain, and focuses on guidance for the resumption of operations following an all hazards incident.[15] The strategy aims to integrate the many plans and initiatives currently in place in order to secure the supply chain (USDHS 2007).

---

[14] A final version of this strategy is scheduled to be completed by October 2009.

[15] An all hazards incident refers to any incident, terrorist or natural disaster, that could affect the maritime transportation system.

TABLE 9

Overview of Major Federal Programs for Supply Chain Security

Throughout the Supply Chain	Port of Origin	Port of Origin to the U.S. Port of Entry	U.S. Port of Entry	Port of Entry to Destination
C-TPAT (Customs-Trade Partnership Against Terrorism)	CSI (Container Security Initiative)	The International Ship and Port Facility Security Code (ISPS Code)	Advance notice of arrival	Certain dangerous cargo tracking
CSDs (Container Security Devices)	SFI (Secure Freight Initiative)	MDA (Maritime Domain Awareness)	Operational security measures	Highway security
	ATS (Automated Targeting Systems)	NAIS (Nationwide Automatic Identification System)	Maritime security regulations	Rail security
	DOE Megaports Initiative	LRIT (Long Range Identification and Tracking of Vessels)	Transportation Worker Identification Credential (TWIC)	Air cargo security
	TSA Known Shipper Database International Port Security Program		CBP cargo screening NII (non-intrusive inspection) and radiation scanning technology	

SOURCE: U.S. Department of Homeland Security, Draft Strategy to Enhance International Supply Chain Security, July 2007.

USDHS and its partners have programs in place to secure maritime cargo throughout the chain of custody, from the origination of the cargo through its arrival at a final destination (Frittelli 2002). Table 9 provides an overview of federal programs to secure the various points in the maritime supply chain. Each program in this table has a unique responsibility in maritime cargo security and takes a specific approach to it.

Customs-Trade Partnership Against Terrorism (C-TPAT) is a voluntary public-private partnership program in which the private owners of supply chain infrastructure and cargo work with U.S. Customs and Border Protection (CBP) to improve the security of the international supply chain. C-TPAT participants are asked to ensure that their own security plans and practices are in compliance with C-TPAT security criteria and coordinated with their business partners throughout the supply chain. CBP validates and regularly revalidates an entity's participation in C-TPAT (USDHS 2007). As of March 2008, C-TPAT had more than 8,200 certified members. C-TPAT members account for 80 percent of the value of goods imported into the United States (USDHS CBP 2008).

The Secure Freight Initiative (SFI), a joint program of USDHS and the U.S. Department of Energy (USDOE), is implemented by CBP and USDOE. SFI began as a pilot program in which seven overseas ports participated in scanning all U.S.-bound containers for nuclear or radiological materials. The SFI pilot phase was intended to help authorities prepare for the scanning of U.S.-bound containers that will be required in the future (GAO 2008b). In the pilot phase, however, 100 percent of container cargo was scanned at just three of the seven participating ports: Port Qasim, Karachi, Pakistan; Puerto Cortes, Honduras; and Southampton, United Kingdom (USDHS CBP 2007a).

SFI builds on the Container Security Initiative (CSI), a CBP program, which works with foreign governments and cargo and facility owners to target and inspect high-risk cargo at its port of origin. SFI also builds on the USDOE's Megaports Initiative, which works with partner governments to scan containers for nuclear or radioactive materials (USDHS CBP 2007b).

In addition to these programs, the Transportation Security Administration (TSA) began distributing individual port security grants in 2002. By fiscal year 2005, grants awarded totaled $632 million. Grants have aided ports in conducting security assessments, enhancing facility or operational security, and implementing cutting-edge technology (Haveman et al. 2006).

SPOTLIGHT 3: PORTS AND ENVIRONMENTAL CONCERNS

Oceanborne container activities at U.S. seaports, while essential for trade and commerce, can affect water quality, air quality, and land-use patterns. The complex interconnections between port activities and environmental quality have implications for the nation's coastal, ocean, and freshwater resources. They also affect transportation demands and traffic congestion. U.S. ports have recently renewed their attention to environmental concerns. In particular, port and federal agencies with responsibility for marine environmental quality have focused on the following issues:

- Water quality. The greater use of larger shipping vessels and increased portside traffic escalate the risk both of introducing nonindigenous aquatic species through ballast water[16] and of leaking of toxic materials into marine ecosystems. They also increase demand for dredging of sediments in ports and harbors.

- Air quality. Increased container activity and the accompanying growth in truck and cargo-handling equipment operating at U.S. ports generate additional air pollutants, including carbon monoxide (CO), ozone (O_3), nitrogen oxide (NO_2), and sulfur dioxide (SO_2). Port activities can also result in noise pollution.

- Land-use patterns. Increased containership traffic and activity at ports adds to traffic congestion around the ports, affecting landside access. Because port traffic intermingles with residential and commercial traffic in the adjacent land areas, growth in container traffic results in increasing congestion for both freight carriers and private citizens.

U.S. ports are also considering the potential environmental challenges implicit in climate change, including costs of improved infrastructure to protect harbors from rising sea levels, increased port maintenance costs, and increased operations costs due to delays in shipping activities (EPA 2008b).

To deal with these challenges, the U.S. Environmental Protection Agency (EPA) has introduced new environmental and sustainability initiatives. EPA's initiative to reduce diesel emissions at U.S. ports, called Clean Ports USA, suggests a variety of operational and technological ideas that ports can adapt to their individual needs, including truck idle reduction, the use of cleaner fuel, and replacement of older equipment (EPA 2005). EPA has also developed an overarching strategy for sustainable ports that provides measures that ports can implement, largely voluntarily, in partnership with the agency. Focus areas include clean air and affordable energy, clean and safe water, healthy communities and ecosystems, the global environment, ports communication, and enforcement (EPA 2007).

By 2008, more than 18 U.S. ports were developing and using Environmental Management Systems (EMS), which integrate environmental considerations in both day-to-day operational decisions and long-term planning (EPA 2008a). Many U.S. ports have also launched their own "green" initiatives. For example, the ports of Los Angeles and Long Beach have received national attention for environmental efforts focused on air quality. With help from California state and local air-quality agencies, for example, they are using cleaner fuels and replacing older trucks with hybrid vehicles, including the world's first hybrid tugboat (Murr 2008).

---

[16] Ballast water is taken on empty ships to stabalize the ship. When a ship is loaded with cargo, the ballast water is pumped out, introducing aquatic organisms from its origin port at its destination.

References

American Trucking Association (ATA). 2009. Historical Trucking Index Database, as of Mar. 25, 2009. Personal communication.

Association of American Railroads (AAR). 2008. *Rail Intermodal Transportation*. Available at www.aar.org, as of Mar. 31, 2009.

Association of American Railroads (AAR). 2009. *Class I Railroad Statistics 2009*. Available at www.aar.org/Resources/Resources%20Landing.aspx, as of Mar. 20, 2009.

AXS-Alphaliner. 2009. *AXS-Alphaliner Newsletter*, no. 2009/09. Available at www.alphaliner.com, as of Mar. 5, 2009.

Cohen, S.S. 2006. Boom Boxes: Containers and Terrorism. In *Protecting the Nation's Seaports: Balancing Security and Cost*. Edited by J.D. Haveman and H.J. Shatz. San Francisco: Public Policy Institute of California.

Dennis, B. Too Many Cars and They're Not on the Road: After 'Car Bubble' Collapses, Excess Inventory Creates a Backlog. *The Washington Post*, Apr. 3, 2009, A1.

Frittelli, J. 2002. *Maritime Security: Overview of Issues*. Congressional Research Service (CRS) Report for Congress. Washington, DC.

Haveman, J.D., H.J. Shatz, and E. Vilchis. 2006. The Government Response: U.S. Port Security Programs. In *Protecting the Nation's Seaports: Balancing Security and Cost*. Edited by J.D. Haveman and H.J. Shatz. San Francisco: Public Policy Institute of California.

ICC Commercial Crime Services. 2009. Somali Pirates Take Two Container Ships off the East Coast of Somalia. News, April 8. Available at www.icc-ccs.org, as of Apr. 8, 2009.

Intermodal Association of North America. 2008. *Rail Intermodal Traffic Activity—2008*. Available at www.intermodal.org/statistics_files/stats6.shtml, as of Mar. 16, 2009.

The Journal of Commerce (JOC). 2009a. Port Import Export Reporting Service (PIERS). Available at The Journal of Commerce Online, www.joc.com, as of Mar. 20, 2009.

The Journal of Commerce (JOC). 2009b. Port Import Export Reporting Service (PIERS), Annual Container Trade Data. Available at The Journal of Commerce Online, www.joc.com, as of Mar. 20, 2009.

Leach, P.T. 2009. Auto Sprawl. *The Journal of Commerce* 10, no. 9 (Mar. 2): 24–26.

Mongelluzzo, B. 2008. How to Find an Export Box. *The Journal of Commerce Online*, June 30. Available at www.joc.com/node/403939.

Murr, A. 2008. Shipping News: The "Greening" of America's Two Biggest Ports. *Newsweek* (Web exclusive), September 9. Available at www.newsweek.com/id/158126, as of Apr. 7, 2009.

National Research Council (NRC), Transportation Research Board (TRB). 2003. *Special Report 271: Freight Capacity for the 21st Century*. Washington, DC.

National Surface Transportation Policy and Revenue Study Commission. 2007. *Transportation for Tomorrow: Report of the National Surface Transportation Policy and Revenue Study Commission*. Washington, DC. Available at http://transportationfortomorrow.org, as of Mar. 31, 2009.

New York Times. 2009. Times Topics: Piracy at Sea. Available at http://topics.nytimes.com/top/reference/timestopics/subjects/p/piracy_at_sea/index.html, as of Apr. 8, 2009.

Organisation for Economic Co-operation and Development (OECD), Directorate for Science, Technology and Industry, Maritime Transport Committee. 2003. *Security in Maritime Transport: Risk Factors and Economic Impact*. Paris, France. July.

The Port Authority of New York/New Jersey (PANYNJ). 2009. Press release, March 20, 2009. Available at www.panynj.gov/AboutthePortAuthority/PressCenter/PressReleases/PressRelease/index.php?id=1212, as of Mar. 20, 2009.

Union Pacific Corp. 2009. *Annual Report to the U.S. Securities and Exchange Commission*, Feb. 6. Available at www.up.com/investors/attachments/secfiling/2009/upc10k_020609.pdf, as of Mar. 16, 2009.

U.S. Department of Commerce (USDOC), Bureau of Economic Analysis (BEA). 2009. *Gross Domestic Product: Fourth Quarter 2008* (Final). News release, Mar. 26. Available at www.bea.gov/newsreleases/national/gdp/gdpnewsrelease.htm.

U.S. Department of Commerce (USDOC), Census Bureau (CB) and Bureau of Economic Analysis (BEA). 2009. *U.S. International Trade in Goods and Services* (December 2008). Press release, Feb. 11. Available at www.census.gov/foreign-trade/Press-Release/2008pr/12.

U.S. Department of Commerce (USDOC), Census Bureau (CB), Division of Foreign Trade, 2009. Available at www.census.gov/foreign-trade, as of Mar. 30, 2009.

U.S. Department of Homeland Security (USDHS). 2007. *Strategy to Enhance International Supply Chain Security.* Washington, DC. July. Available at www.dhs.gov, as of Mar. 31, 2009.

U.S. Department of Homeland Security (USDHS), Customs and Border Protection (CBP). 2006. *Fact Sheet: An Overall Picture of Port Security.* July 12. Available at www.cbp.gov, as of Mar. 31, 2009.

U.S. Department of Homeland Security (USDHS), Customs and Border Protection (CBP). 2007a. *Fact Sheet: Secure Freight Scanning at a Glance.* October 11. Available at www.cbp.gov, as of Mar. 31, 2009.

U.S. Department of Homeland Security (USDHS), Customs and Border Protection (CBP). 2007b. *Fact Sheet: Secure Freight with CSI, Megaports.* October 11. Available at www.cbp.gov, as of Mar. 31, 2009.

U.S. Department of Homeland Security (USDHS), Customs and Border Protection (CBP). 2008. *Fact Sheet: C-TPAT.* March 27. Available at www.cbp.gov, as of Mar. 31, 2009.

U.S. Department of Homeland Security (USDHS), Customs and Border Protection (CBP), Mission Support Services. 2009. Operations Management Database, as of Mar. 20, 2009. Personal communication.

U.S. Department of Transportation (USDOT), Federal Highway Administration (FHWA). 2000. *NHS Intermodal Freight Connectors: A Report to Congress.* Washington, DC. December.

U.S. Department of Transportation (USDOT), Federal Highway Administration (FHWA). 2008. *Freight Story 2008.* Washington, DC. Available at http://ops.fhwa.dot.gov/freight/freight_analysis/freight_story, as of Apr. 7, 2009.

U.S. Department of Transportation (USDOT), Maritime Administration (MARAD). 2005. *Report to Congress on the Performance of Ports and the Intermodal System.* Washington, DC. Available at http://marad.dot.gov/documents/Rpt_to_Congress-Perf_Ports_Intermodal_Sys-June2005.pdf, as of Apr. 7, 1009.

U.S. Department of Transportation (USDOT), Research and Innovative Technology Administration (RITA), Bureau of Transportation Statistics (BTS). 2009. Transportation Services Index press release, as of Jan. 20, 2009.

U.S. Environmental Protection Agency (EPA). 2005. *Clean Ports USA: Navigating Toward Cleaner Air.* Washington, DC. November. Available at www.epa.gov/otaq/diesel/ports/documents/420f05033.pdf, as of Apr. 7, 2009.

U.S. Environmental Protection Agency (EPA). 2007. EPA Strategy for Sustainable Ports. September 6. Available at www.epa.gov/ispd/ports/index.html, as of Apr. 7, 2009.

U.S. Environmental Protection Agency (EPA). 2008a. *An Environmental Management System (EMS) Primer for Ports: Advancing Port Sustainability.* Washington, DC. Jan. 4. Available at www.epa.gov/ispd/ports/emsprimer.pdf, as of Apr. 7, 2009.

U.S. Environmental Protection Agency (EPA). 2008b. *Planning for Climate Change Impacts at U.S. Ports.* White paper. Washington, DC. July. Available at www.epa.gov/ispd/ports/ports-planing-for-cci-white-paper.pdf, as of Apr. 7, 2009.

U.S. Government Accountability Office (GAO). 2008a. Letter to Rep. James L. Oberstar and Rep. Peter A. DeFazio: *Approaches to Mitigate Freight Congestion,* Nov. 20. Available at www.gao.gov/products/GAO-09-163R, as of Apr. 7, 2009.

U.S. Government Accountability Office (GAO). 2008b. *Supply Chain Security: Challenges to Scanning 100 Percent of U.S.-Bound Cargo Containers.* Washington, DC. . Available at www.gao.gov, as of Mar. 31, 2009.

World Trade Organization (WTO), 2008. *World Trade Report 2008.* Available at http://www.wto.org/english/res_e/reser_e/wtr_e.htm, as of Mar. 1, 2009.

List of Abbreviations

AAR	Association of American Railroads
ATA	American Trucking Association
BEA	Bureau of Economic Analysis
BTS	Bureau of Transportation Statistics
CB	U.S. Census Bureau
CBP	U.S. Customs and Border Protection
dwt	deadweight tons
EPA	U.S. Environmental Protection Agency
FHWA	Federal Highway Administration
FRA	Federal Railroad Administration
GAO	U.S. Government Accountability Office
GDP	gross domestic product
GHG	greenhouse gas
ICC	International Chamber of Commerce
MARAD	Maritime Administration
OECD	Organisation for Economic Co-operation and Development
RITA	Research and Innovative Technology Administration
TEU	twenty-foot equivalent container unit
TSA	Transportation Security Administration
TTI	Texas Transportation Institute
USCG	U.S. Coast Guard
USDHS	U.S. Department of Homeland Security
USDOC	U.S. Department of Commerce
USDOE	U.S. Department of Energy
USDOT	U.S. Department of Transportation

Glossary

Definitions in this glossary are adapted from the U.S. Department of Transportation, Research and Innovative Technologies Administration, Bureau of Transportation Statistics, available at www.bts. gov/dictionary.

All hazards incident. Refers to any incident, the result of terrorism or a natural disaster, that could affect the maritime transportation system.

Ballast water. Fresh or salt water, sometimes containing sediments, held in tanks and cargo holds of ships to increase stability and maneuverability during transit.

Break-bulk. Packages of maritime cargo that are handled individually, palletized, or unitized for purposes of transportation as opposed to bulk and containerized freight.

Bulk carrier. A ship with specialized holds for carrying dry or liquid commodities, such as oil, grain, ore, and coal, in unpackaged bulk form. Bulk carriers may be designed to carry a single bulk product (crude oil tanker) or accommodate several bulk product types (ore/bulk/oil carrier) on the same voyage or on a subsequent voyage after holds are cleaned.

Chained dollars. A measure used to express real prices, defined as prices that are adjusted to remove the effect of changes in the purchasing power of the dollar. Real prices usually reflect buying power relative to a reference year. The "chained-dollar" measure is based on the average weights of goods and services in successive pairs of years. It is "chained" because the second year in each pair, with its weights, becomes the first year of the next pair. Before 1996, real prices were expressed in constant dollars, a weighted measure of goods and services in a single year. See also *current dollars*.

Class I freight railroad. Defined by the American Association of Railroads each year based on annual operating revenue. For 2008, the threshold for Class I railroads was revenues exceeding $360 million. A railroad is dropped from the Class I list if it fails to meet the annual revenue threshold for three consecutive years.

Container. A large standard-size metal box into which cargo is packed for shipment aboard specially configured oceangoing containerships. It is designed to be moved with common handling equipment to enable high-speed intermodal transfers in economically large units between ships, railcars, truck chassis, and barges using a minimum of labor. Therefore, the container rather than the cargo in it serves as the transfer unit.

Containerization. A system of intermodal freight transportation that uses standard containers that can be loaded onto vessels, railcars, and trucks. It involves the stowage of general or special cargo in a container for transport in the various modes.

Containership. A cargo vessel designed and constructed to transport, within specifically designed cells, portable tanks and freight containers, which are lifted on and off with their contents intact.

Containerized cargo: Cargo that is practical to transport in a container and results in a more economical shipment than could be achieved by shipping the cargo in some other form of unitization (e.g., break-bulk).

Container terminal. An area designated for the stowage of cargo in containers. It is usually accessible by truck, railroad, and marine transportation. At a container terminal, containers are picked up, dropped off, maintained, and housed.

Container throughput. A measure of the number of containers handled over a period of time. It is a standard measure for the productivity of a seaport. Container throughput is measured by twenty-foot equivalent units (TEU).

Current dollars. Dollar value of a good or service in terms of prices current at the time the good or service is sold. See also *chained dollars*.

Customs-Trade Partnership Against Terrorism (C-TPAT). A voluntary public-private partnership program in which the private owners of supply chain infrastructure and cargo work with U.S. Customs and Border Protection to improve the security of the international supply chain. See www.cbp.gov for details.

Deadweight tons (dwt). The total weight of a ship's load, including cargo, fuel, and crew. The deadweight tonnage of a ship is the difference between its weight when completely empty and its weight when fully loaded.

Gross domestic product (GDP). The total value of goods and services produced by labor and property located in the United States. As long as the labor and property are located in the United States, the supplier (the workers and, for property, the owners) may be either U.S. residents or residents of foreign countries.

Highway-rail crossing. A location where one or more railroad tracks intersect a public or private thoroughfare, a sidewalk, or a pathway.

Intermodal container. A freight container designed to permit it to be used interchangeably in two or more modes of transport.

Intermodal. Used to denote movements of cargo containers interchangeably between transport modes—i.e., motor, water, and air carriers—and where the equipment is compatible within the multiple systems.

Just in time (JIT). A method of inventory control in which warehousing is minimal or nonexistent. A container is the movable warehouse and must arrive "just in time," not too early or too late.

Marine terminal. A designated area of a port used for the transmission, care, and convenience of cargo and/or passengers in the interchange of them between land and water carriers or between two water carriers. It includes wharves, warehouses, covered and/or open storage spaces, cold storage plants, grain elevators and/or bulk cargo loading and/or unloading structures, landings, and receiving stations.

Marine Transportation System (MTS). Consists of all the intermodal components that are part of the maritime domain, including ships, ports, inland waterways, intermodal rail and truck, and other users of the maritime system.

Merchandise trade exports. Merchandise transported out of the United States to foreign countries whether such merchandise is exported from within the U.S. Customs Service territory, from a U.S. Customs bonded warehouse, or from a U.S. Foreign Trade Zone. (Foreign Trade Zones are areas, operated as public utilities, under the control of U.S. Customs with facilities for handling, storing, manipulating, manufacturing, and exhibiting goods.)

Merchandise trade imports. Commodities of foreign origin entering the United States, as well as goods of domestic origin returned to the United States with no change in condition or after having been processed and/or assembled in other countries. Puerto Rico is a customs district within the U.S. Customs territory, and its trade with foreign countries is included in U.S. import statistics. U.S. import statistics also include merchandise trade between the U.S. Virgin Islands and foreign countries even though the islands are not officially a part of the U.S. Customs territory.

Port. A harbor area in which marine terminal facilities for transferring cargo between ships and land transportation are located.

Real gross domestic product (GDP). The real counterpart to current/nominal GDP, obtained by valuing output in a given year at prices from another year, called the base year. It reflects correction for inflation and changes in the price of goods and services.

Roll-on/roll-off vessel. Ships that are designed to carry wheeled containers or other wheeled cargo and that use the roll-on/roll-off method for loading and unloading.

Secure Freight Initiative (SFI). A joint program of the U.S. Department of Homeland Security and the U.S. Department of Energy that is designed to scan U.S.-bound containers for nuclear or radiological materials at their foreign ports of origin. See www.cbp.gov/xp/cgov/trade/cargo_security/secure_freight_initiative for details.

Tanker. An oceangoing ship designed to haul liquid bulk cargo in world trade.

Twenty-foot equivalent unit (TEU). The standard unit for measuring the volume of containers that seaports handle. Standard container sizes are 20 feet, 40 feet, and 48 feet long.

Virtual container yard. Virtual container yards are Web-based platforms where users can match empty containers to container needs at the dock rather than returning them to the terminal.

Other recent BTS maritime-related reports

Maritime Trade & Transportation 2007 provides an update on the major marine infrastructure, maritime-related transportation services, domestic and international freight and passenger trade, the economic impact of the Maritime Transportation System, safety and environment, national security, and shipbuilding. It also presents information about the St. Lawrence Seaway and the U.S. Coast Guard (92 pages, 2008).

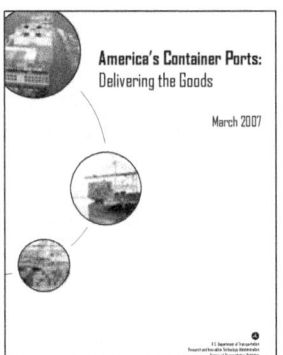

America's Container Ports: Delivering the Goods 2007 examines trends in U.S. containerized cargo and freight activity at major U.S. container ports. It reviews the direction of container traffic, port concentration, regional port trends, vessel calls and capacity, trading patterns, and container entries by all modes (11 pages, 2007).